Psychoanalysis as a Subversive Phenomenon

Psychoanalytic Studies: Clinical, Social, and Cultural Contexts

Series Editor
Michael O'Loughlin, Adelphi University

Mission Statement

Psychoanalytic Studies seeks psychoanalytically informed works addressing the implications of the location of the individual in clinical, social, cultural, historical, and ideological contexts. Innovative theoretical and clinical works within psychoanalytic theory and in fields such as anthropology, education, and history are welcome. Projects addressing conflict, migrations, difference, ideology, subjectivity, memory, psychiatric suffering, physical and symbolic violence, power, and the future of psychoanalysis itself are welcome, as are works illustrating critical and activist applications of clinical work.

See https://rowman.com/Action/SERIES/LEX/LEXPS for a list of advisory board members.

Titles in the Series

Psychoanalysis as a Subversive Phenomenon: Social Change, Virtue Ethics, and Analytic Theory, by Amber M. Trotter
A People's History of Psychoanalysis: From Freud to Liberation Psychology, by Daniel José Gaztambide
Rethinking the Relation between Women and Psychoanalysis: Loss, Mourning, and the Feminine, edited by Hada Soria Escalante
Lives Interrupted: Psychiatric Narratives of Struggle and Resilience, edited by Michael O'Loughlin, Secil Arac-Orhun, and Montana Queler
Women and the Psychosocial Construction of Madness, edited by Marie Brown and Marilyn Charles
Revisioning War Trauma in Cinema: Uncoming Communities, by Jessica Datema and Manya Steinkoler
Women & Psychosis: Multidisciplinary Perspectives, edited by Marie Brown and Marilyn Charles
Psychoanalysis from the Indian Terroir: Emerging Themes in Culture, Family, and Childhood in India, edited by Manasi Kumar, Anup Dhar, and Anurag Mishra
A Three-Factor Model of Couples Therapy: Projective Identification, Couple Object Relations, and Omnipotent Control, by Robert Mendelsohn

Psychoanalysis as a Subversive Phenomenon

Social Change, Virtue Ethics, and Analytic Theory

Amber M. Trotter, PhD

LEXINGTON BOOKS
Lanham • Boulder • New York • London

Published by Lexington Books
An imprint of The Rowman & Littlefield Publishing Group, Inc.
4501 Forbes Boulevard, Suite 200, Lanham, Maryland 20706
www.rowman.com

6 Tinworth Street, London SE11 5AL

British Library Cataloguing in Publication Information Available

Library of Congress Cataloging-in-Publication Data Available

ISBN 978-1-4985-7332-0 (cloth)
ISBN 978-1-4985-7333-7 (electronic)

Contents

Acknowledgments

A special thank you to Andy Harlem—without your unfailing support and erudition, this project would not exist. Thank you for trusting me, for challenging me, and for showing me what it is to be an outstanding teacher. Michael O'Loughlin's thoughtful and generous feedback on the dissertation from which this book came has been instrumental to my thinking. Thank you for sharing your scholarship and skillful editing. Thank you to Michael Guy Thompson for fostering my developing understanding of psychoanalysis and subversion; to Peter Carnochan helping me to bring more of myself to my work; to Lani Chow, Bart Magee, Ruth Simon, Adam Blum, and my patients and colleagues for teaching me to be a therapist; to the members of the Society for Psychoanalytic Inquiry, from whom I have learned so much; and to Kasey Beduhn and Lexington Books for publishing the present work. Finally, thank you to my parents for teaching me to think critically and passionately from an early age, and to my husband—your love and patience have been the soil and sunlight of my adult development.

Introduction

This book considers psychoanalysis as a potentially subversive phenomenon. I am intrigued by psychoanalysis's legacy of radical sociopolitical application. Psychoanalysis's liminal position, set both within and in opposition to hegemonic Western culture, its critical engagement with subjectivity and truth, its insistence on honesty, freedom, and privacy, its exposition of unconscious processes, and insights into the relationship between individuals, families, and states compels me. I *want* to see psychoanalysis as subversive. Yet I feel skeptical, disheartened by divisiveness, myopia, passivity, and conformity within the field, as well as the marginalization of analytic ideas and therapy in contemporary society. I find myself agreeing with theorists who celebrate psychoanalysis's essential radical spirit, as well as with those who lament its perpetuation of oppressive social norms and gradual dissolution.

Those seeking disruptive countercultural dimensions of psychoanalysis find ample evidence, both in terms of intrinsic qualities and historical application. At its inception, psychoanalysis presented a novel conceptualization of the human psyche, and an affront to hegemonic Victorian views (Aron & Starr, 2013; Danto, 2005; Lear, 1998; Zaretsky, 2015). Freud's insights laid bare a psyche driven by unconscious conflict, repressed desires, and impulsive cravings—a psyche making significant decisions on the basis of subjective and idiosyncratic feelings and biases, rather than logical objective facts (Thompson, 1995). Freud's clinical work demonstrated plainly that "the intellect is a relatively weak player in the theater of the mind" (Carnochan, 2001, p. 100). Freud asserted, moreover, that irrational, unconscious behavior was not merely arbitrary, but rather obeyed a hidden logic of its own (Lear, 1998). Although Freud was in many ways an Enlightenment thinker—certainly, he considered himself to be—his theories in fact subverted prevailing epistemological claims. Analytic theory suggests that we can best approach some things, such as greater self-knowledge, obliquely, that truth is dynamic and contextual, and that mystery pervades experience. Even in our post-postmodern world, this contradicts the basic premise of Western science: that there is an ultimate observable reality, which we are prevented from fully understanding merely by lack of knowledge, tools, and so on. Psychoanalysis problematizes the project of objective knowing. Analytic theories of unconscious process warn against overconfidence in rational intelligence, force engagement with more mysterious and unsettling dimensions of being, and present a version of truth that is evolving, relational, dialectic, and circumscribed—more process than data (Bollas, 1999; Summers, 2013; Zaretsky, 2015).

Freud further disturbed conceptions of rational egoism through his illumination of our tendency to internalize and reify the social order. Psychoanalysis highlights the systemic reproduction of sociocultural values through family, morality, education, and so on. Freud's exposition of the production of moral sentiments, sexual fantasies, and other private matters through sociocultural and historical processes rattles our sense of our own subjectivity, drawing complex links between individuals and society, and revealing our complicity in our own enslavement (Zaretsky, 2015). Psychoanalysis is as much a theory of society as of psyche, and insights into the interpenetration of psyche and polis have been central to analytic theory's utilization by myriad radical theorists and social movements—including "the cultural rebellions of the 1920s, African American radicalism, surrealism, Popular Front antifascism, the New Left, radical feminism, and queer theory" (Zaretsky, 2015, p. 2). Even as psychoanalysis has disappeared from mainstream psychology programs, Freud's critique of society persistently attracts interest. Works such as "Civilization and Its Discontents" (in which Freud [1930/1961] enumerates the ailments of "modern" society and the fundamentally antithetical relationship between the individual and the state) remain enduringly popular in sociology, critical theory, and philosophy programs (Lear, 1998).

Of course, the psychoanalytic subject is no mere product. Neither autonomous in a full Enlightenment sensibility, nor fully constructed, as in traditional Marxism, the analysand, if radically conditioned, is also radically free. Freud traced processes of systemic reproduction, but also upheld the possibility of relatively autonomous ethical development (Wallwork, 1991). His ideas ultimately affirm an idiosyncratic, creative subject, and the capacity to change through deliberative practice. Psychoanalysis holds open the possibility of real, hard-won changes, promoting "the expansion of the moral capacity while delimiting and contextualizing its scope" (Zaretsky, 2015, p. 189). In an era that increasingly attributes our every affect to genes, behavior, and environment, affirming the eternal possibility of internally driven change—

of free will, if you like, in defiance of fate—is a bold position, perhaps a subversive one (Fong, 2012; Summers, 2013). Through analysis, patients experience not only repressed desires and oppressive internalized cultural prescriptions, but also the possibility of a particular sort of freedom.

Free association, psychoanalysis's signature technique, promotes unpredictable, expansive self-expression. Analysis encourages free speech not in the sense of saying whatever one consciously decides to, but rather in the sense of allowing the convoluted, repressed, and unknown to take form. Free association entails a particular honesty, at once dangerous and liberating (Bollas, 1999; Thompson, 2004). Psychoanalysis forces us to examine our habitual assumptions, latent yearnings, and unpleasant feelings, culturally programmed and otherwise. It draws shadows into the light, often to destabilizing effect. Yet analytic theorists aver that there will always be shadow: no amount of making the unconscious conscious will ever threaten the unconscious existentially. We will never fully understand life, and can no more control ourselves than we can the world.

In the field's early years, the politics of the analytic community largely reflected these seeds of subversion: first-generation analysts, including many Marxists and women, were cultural and political rebels who criticized dominant conceptualizations of sexuality, education, and the relationship between the individual and the state (Aron & Starr, 2013; Jacoby, 1983). Early analysts saw the conditions of the social order reflected in individual symptomology, and thus viewed mental health care as an embodied sociopolitical critique—a sort of activism (Tauber, 2012). They hoped psychoanalysis would both liberate individuals from repressed states and deepen our understanding of the sociopolitical matrix, facilitating change in social conditions. They did not conceive of psychoanalysis as a specialized treatment for the few, but rather advocated free, public psychotherapy clinics (Aron & Starr, 2013; Danto, 2005). Because these analysts postulated complex interrelatedness between individuals and societies, they asserted that social change was integral to relieving human suffering, while also suggesting that such change would require evolution in human subjectivity and values (Jacoby, 1983).

Following this period of early radicalism, left-wing politics and psychoanalysis largely diverged. Psychoanalysis met with forceful repression as Nazi power spread across Europe; the analytic community fractured, with many analysts fleeing to the United States, where suppression of analytic ideas continued under McCarthy-era politics. Radicalism within psychoanalysis met with internal censure as well (Jacoby, 1983). Émigré analysts, traumatized by personal and historical events, were eager to gain a sense of security. An opportunity presented itself in American psychiatry's efforts to reinvent itself in the wake of dead-end institutionalized care and sophisticated new psychotropic medications. Psychoanalysis became virtually synonymous with psychiatry in postwar America—medical degrees became required for analysts, and the professional culture grew more orthodox and elitist. Analytic practitioners enjoyed cultural prestige and economic prosperity for decades, while analytic concepts infiltrated common language (Aron & Starr, 2013).

The period of decline following this "Golden Era" has witnessed acrimonious internal splintering and a pervasive discrediting of psychoanalysis by the scientific mainstream (Aron & Starr, 2013; Stepansky, 2009; Mills, 2012). Despite cutting-edge infant and neuroscientific research upholding much of analytic theory, compelling empirical support for the efficacy of psychodynamic psychotherapy (e.g., Wampold, 2005; Westen, Novotny, & Thompson-Brenner, 2004), and increasing flexibility vis-a-vis schedule, frame, and fee (McWilliams, 2004), the psychological mainstream continues to disparage psychoanalysis as it moves resolutely toward its goal of becoming a STEM discipline (Summers, 2013). Psychoanalysis has been criticized as self-serving on the part of the professional, self-indulgent on the part of the patient, sexist, elitist, capitalist, and just plain crazy (Aron & Starr, 2013; Shedler, 2010).

The effects are stark: a tiny fraction of patients (most of them analysts in training) engage in traditional (3–4x/week) analysis, while a similarly small number of graduate training programs emphasize a psychoanalytic approach. Analytically oriented APA-accredited internships are scarce, while the annual meeting of the American Psychoanalytic Association has been likened to a group of dinosaurs deliberating various routes to extinction (Aron & Starr, 2013).

As psychoanalysis fights for survival, generative subversive sociopolitical critique may appear distal. Across politics, activism, and academia, the vision of psychoanalysis as an indispensable thread of progressive social thought does not appear to have been realized. Neither the general public nor academics without a special interest consider psychoanalysis important to understanding current sociopolitical issues (Lear, 1998; Stepansky, 2009). While academic psychoanalysis does serve a critical function within the humanities, this role is highly circumscribed, and clinical psychoanalysis has largely failed to secure a role in broad progressive discourse (Lear, 1998; Zaretsky, 2015).

Ample blame for psychoanalysis's current status can doubtless be leveled at the psychoanalytic community, and many theorists have done so. Thompson (2004) laments practitioners' insular focus, writing, "It is my impression that psychoanalysis, like an old codger, is dying, and we have no one to blame but ourselves" (p. xix). Kirsner (2000), Mills (2012), and Stepansky (2009) attribute psychoanalysis's decline to a combination of divisive factionalism and hierarchies, stifling orthodoxy, and ontological confusion. Summers (2013), meanwhile, comments that intense pressure to "prove" its efficacy and scientific status has led the analytic community away from radical theory and practice, and toward a certitude antithetical to its essence. That is, the desire to arrive at verifiable, discrete truths about the human psyche, which can be systematically applied, has worked against a subversive psychoanalysis. Despite broadening interest in the application of analytic ideas to broader sociopolitical phenomenon, psychoanalysis focuses largely on individual patients and subjective experience. Philosophical and political positions are often eschewed in the putative service of "neutrality" (Botticelli, 2004; Cushman, 2015). Another angle of critique is that psychoanalysis's history and liberal, individualist, patriarchal, and sexist assumptions make it a bourgeois praxis relevant only to white affluent populations, and obsolete in the context of contemporary multicultural radical politics (e.g., Kovel, 1983; Walls, 2004). The divide between clinical and academic psychoanalysis in the United States has only further diminished the field's potential social impact (Lear, 1998). Surely, this is not a picture of subversion.

Yet despite widespread, persistent, often scathing critique, and withering support from mainstream psychology and hegemonic culture prophets of psychoanalysis's demise are repeatedly discredited. Psychoanalysis continues to attract new and diverse generations of thinkers, clinicians, and patients alike (Zepf, 2010). It seems unlikely that psychoanalysis has survived despite sustained sociopolitical slander and economic impracticality merely because it offers one among many forms of effective psychological treatment. Instead, I suspect psychoanalysis survives in part because it offers something unique—and perhaps subversive—with implications beyond the consulting room. If nothing else, the slander and repression repeatedly directed at psychoanalysis accords with the treatment of subversive forces. As Lear (1998) observes, "A battle may be fought over Freud, but the war is over our culture's image of the human soul" (p. 27)—specifically over questions of liberty, irrationality, and unconscious motivation. Perhaps psychoanalysis survives because it obstinately carries a torch of wild freedom and reverence for the unknowable in a world of rational epistemology and increasingly rigid sociopolitical control. Psychoanalysis does not scream its sociopolitical agenda, waving signs and shouting slogans, but may be a fundamentally political project nonetheless, and one of a subversive nature.

Before proceeding to examine psychoanalysis's potentially subversive features more closely, I would like to make a few brief methodological notes. First, psychoanalysis is both a theory and a practice, each with many distinct incubations, and the discipline's basic ontology and epistemology are subject to fierce debate. Chasms can at times exist between opposing theoretical schools, as well as between clinical and academic factions. I do not offer an exclusive definition, but will rather present a working understanding of psychoanalysis as an embodied tradition of thinking about and relating to the human condition. More precisely, I will consider psychoanalysis as a discipline of character—as an ethic in Platonic-Aristotelian terms. The version of psychoanalysis I present is, moreover, a frankly enthusiastic rendering. I do not mean to indicate some fictitious unrealized abstraction—the psychoanalysis I describe derives from my experience as a patient, therapist, and scholar—yet critique is not my central purpose here. Numerous excellent critiques of psychoanalysis exist (e.g., Cushman, 1995; Khanna, 2003; Kirsner, 2000; Kovel, 1981; Mills, 2012; Stepansky, 2009), and I have studied many of them. I hope I do not take up psychoanalysis naively or without acumen, but do describe psychoanalysis in positive terms—a sort of best possible vision.

I do not offer an exhaustive or authoritative account of subversive social change, either—another complex and contested phenomenon with myriad interlocking and dynamic variables. Instead, I draw on social theory to present a case for a conception of subversive processes that emphasizes disruptive ethical engagement.

Finally, I do not answer the question of psychoanalysis's subversiveness conclusively. In fact, I believe, as I have already suggested, that psychoanalysis can be both counted and discounted as a subversive phenomenon. This book can thus most accurately be seen to provide a consideration of this "bothness." It explores psychoanalysis as a subversive phenomenon in terms of both intrinsic qualities and actual engagement, asking questions about gaps between psychoanalysis's subversive potential and its achieved impacts.

Chapter One

Subversion

Examining psychoanalysis as a subversive phenomenon requires an exploration of subversion itself. Subversive phenomenon—distinct from both historically revolutionary and contemporarily countercultural movements—fundamentally disrupt or pervert a prevailing status quo. Subversive forces alter the way things are. Etymologically, *subvertere* means to overturn, or to overthrow from beneath or below (*sub-*, underneath / below + *vertere*, to turn).[1] There is a turning over—by implication a turning over of something—which happens in a particular way.

While in broad terms, subversive processes might disturb any established system or particular status quo, in popular connotation, subversion involves a disruption of prevailing sociopolitical relations—meaning all formal and informal personal, political, and economic associations between people, encompassing both structure and quality. Although often discussed abstractly, sociopolitical relations manifest in the inmost recesses of our daily lives. "Sociopolitical relations" has become a particularly inclusive term in contemporary society, where divisions between work and home, public and private, have become blurred. Advanced capitalist society increasingly erodes private spheres once held to be meaningfully distinct from broader sociopolitical forces while simultaneously dismantling functional public spaces (Arendt, 1958; Habermas, 1989). Such an inclusive understanding of sociopolitical relations highlights the analytic insight that individuals internalize and replicate the sociopolitical order in their day-to-day interactions, while the subjective values and experiences of individual members of society simultaneously manifest in a society's political and economic arrangements. Given the breadth and complexity of sociopolitical relations, potential means of disruption proliferate, and would vary with varying circumstances. A specifically *subversive* disruption of sociopolitical relations, however, would have distinctive features.

To begin with, subversion connotates stealth. While subversive processes do counter prevailing culture, they often do so subtly—even inadvertently or unconsciously. While subversion can certainly be deliberate, it involves less frontal attack, more foundational erosion. Subversive processes also unfold *inside* a given system, proceeding in dialogue with the mainstream. That is, subversion is not a takeover from above or outside, but rather a disruption that develops gradually from within, destabilizing a particular status quo from an intimate perspective. Finally, for all its frequent subtlety, subversion entails fundamental change. Subversive phenomena disturb the existing order at its very roots.

DISRUPTING THE SOCIOPOLITICAL STATUS QUO AT ITS ROOTS

Subversive forces disrupt a given homeostasis, philosophy, way of being—or, most commonly, system of sociopolitical relations. The complex and synergistic nature of sociopolitical relations makes processes of social change highly complicated. Variables proliferate, interact heterogeneously, and vary through history and across cultures. It is perhaps impossible to determine what, exactly, has led to the alteration of a particular sociopolitical paradigm, even in retrospect—much less prospectively.

That said, theories of social change can be roughly divided into "materialist" and "idealist" camps. Materialist theories emphasize structural and mechanistic forces including political process and opportunities, resource mobilization, demographics, economics, changing institutions, and technological advances. In this view, changing material circumstances (e.g., "The Industrial Revolution," "climate change," "technology") drive foundational changes in the social order. By contrast, idealist or ideological theories emphasize more subjective and ineffable variables such as personal and collective identities, interpretation of power relations, and cultural myths, narratives, and values, all of which are seen to influence perception and ultimately action (Hutchinson, 2012; Pulcini, 2013; Weber, 1904/2001). Here, ideology (e.g., "Protestantism," "feminism," "neoliberalism") fundamentally drives social change. New concepts yield new possibilities. What we can imagine shapes what we can create.

These perspectives are not mutually exclusive, but rather a dialectic interaction. Understanding social change demands exploration of both material and ideal variables, independently and in interaction. To neglect one or the other, or their complex bidirectional influence, is to fail, catastrophically, as a social thinker (Reich, 1933/1970). To illustrate the mutual impact of material and ideological forces, consider the political ascendancy of Donald Trump in the United States. In grossly simplified and schematic terms, material factors such as chronic economic difficulties, a global refugee and migration crisis, political corruption, and the inordinate influence of a wealthy elite impacted perceptions, values, and ideology, inflaming racial resentment, xenophobia, and hostility toward established institutions such as the government and the press. Meanwhile these idealist variables impacted the material conditions of daily life, including political leadership, freedom of movement, reproductive rights, taxation, and so on. Cleaving material from ideal factors is artificial—helpful, perhaps, in understanding society, but phenomenologically inaccurate. Life in any given society or culture is a total experience of customs, values, rituals, tools, skills, relationships, opportunities and so on (Heidegger, 1927/1962).

The totality of culture and the interpenetration of materialist and idealist variables notwithstanding, materialist and idealist theories differ in their understanding of the fundamental origins of social change. This is important to the question of subversion, as subversion entails overturning a given system at its roots. Materialist theorists situate structural and systemic variables, such as changing demographics, scarcity of natural resources, economic circumstances, and technological advances as primary, perpetuating secondary changes in ideology. Idealist theorists, by contrast, suggest that our values and perspectives pivotally impact the development, maintenance, and evolution of sociopolitical relations (Hutchinson, 2012; Mason, 2018). What we care about, the stories we tell, and the meaning we make of our lives and world is vital to social change. Relative satisfaction with the dominant paradigm, interpretation of external events, relationships with other people, and the capacity to conceptualize and articulate possible alternative ways of being profoundly influence sociopolitical engagement (The Free Association, 2011; Hutchinson, 2012; Mindell, 2002). From this perspective, disruption of prevailing sociopolitical relations entails disturbing core values, beliefs, and perceptions. I will elaborate a case for this idealist perspective, specifically emphasizing ethics as foundational to social change. This by no means diminishes the importance of material factors, nor the ultimate inseparability of material and ideal factors. However, materialist and idealist theories do approach the foundations of society and processes of change distinctly.

My reasons for focusing on ethics are multiple. To begin with, idealist variables appear particularly important in the contemporary United States, where lifestyle and identity politics and ideological and religious conviction often trump substantive material concerns. Political decisions are increasingly driven by who we think we are—by symbols, rather than issues (Hawkes, 2003; Mason, 2018). The United States has always, arguably, been a nation of believers, deeply invested in our beliefs. The hunger of early Protestant Pilgrim's for the freedom to believe has had a defining influence on

American politics. Further, the persistence of advanced capitalism in light of its staggering and widespread damage has become difficult to explain through material analysis alone. While certainly current economic circumstances are perpetuated by structural coercion, the ideology of late-stage capitalism has become so deeply ingrained that it is reflexive. The logic of TINA (There Is No Alternative) coopts and neutralizes alternative thought (Fisher, 2009). Viable progressive projects and politicians struggle to mobilize meaningful support. Under such circumstances, ideology and ethics become particularly salient: compelling alternatives are required to think our way out of the prevailing status quo (Chibber, 2016; Hawkes, 2003; Streeck, 2017). Furthermore, this project focuses on psychoanalysis, which has little chance of disturbing basic material circumstances, but which may help disrupt prevailing ideology—a question that will be taken up at length in the following chapters.

Important distinctions exist between terms and theories within the broader idealist paradigm. I believe, however, that "ethics," in the Platonic-Aristotelian tradition, captures the essence of the idealist paradigm, while also circumventing some of its limitations. Specifically, this understanding of ethics transcends psychological-sociological bifurcation, conceptualizing the individual subject as both autonomous and constructed, and ideology as both systemically reproduced and idiosyncratically learned. Further, the Platonic tradition conceptualizes ethics as fundamentally embodied, which guards against divisions between theory and action.

In contrast to deontological and consequentialist paradigms, Platonic-Aristotelian or virtue ethics indicates an embodied, dynamic philosophical conception of human flourishing, including suffering and its relief, with both personal and collective, as well as conscious and unconscious, dimensions. Platonic-Aristotelian ethics involves a fundamental vision of what it means to be human and to live life well, as identified and embodied by a particular individual, group, or theory. Ethics in this sense can be conceptualized as pre-political, the often unconscious soil in which political decisions grow. Ethics constitute a response to the eternal Socratic question, "How should I live?"

Any given individual's answer is inevitably shaped by family and culture, including prevailing ideology, but is also intensely personal, and demonstrative of personal responsibility: virtue ethics is a discipline of character. Like character, ethics manifest in and are shaped by daily lived experience and material circumstances, especially relationships of close proximity; there can be no ethics, in this view, in purely abstract terms. Ethics are alive, responsive, and materially situated. They require contact and cannot be determined a priori.

In the absence of concerted effort, one's ethical compass can easily become a reactive emotionality. Ethical commitments are often latent, influencing our behavior at a level below language, and are not especially amenable to change (MacIntyre, 1981). Yet ethics, ideally, though situated in particular lived experience, are directed toward the universal. As a philosophy of praxis, ethics are both aspirational and descriptive, rooted in common practices, habits, and ways of being, but also in broad philosophical principles and theoretical claims. Ethics translate into politics (Critchley, 2007). Although theories of virtue ethics focus on the individual, the presence of the other constitutes the grounds upon which ethics as a discipline becomes necessary: without a collective dimension virtue ethics becomes merely subjective, and thus arbitrary and inept (MacIntyre, 1981). The question "How should I live?" contains "What sort of society do I want to live in?" (Critchley, 2007).

Because ethics, in this view, are nuanced, latent, and dynamic, they can be hard to apprehend. The ethics of a particular culture, institution, theory, or individual can be inferred from its core commitments and principles—its ideology,[2] central customs or habits, its rhetoric, its theory of good and bad—hence the name "Virtue Ethics."

The salience of what I will henceforth call "ethics" to sociopolitical arrangements has long been theorized. Plato, for instance, conceived the "polis" as humankind's creation, requiring individuals to buy into its ethical precepts in order to persist; he thus promoted critical self-examination as a remedy for social ills. Ethics did not become a serious aspect of contemporary academic sociology until the early twentieth century, however, when Weber (1904/2001) argued persuasively that shifting ethical values (namely, the novel Protestant valuation of labor in a calling) was indispensable in the rise of modern capitalism. By locating ethics at the root or core of social change, Weber contradicted the prevailing view that structural, technological, or demographic factors drove the rise of capitalism. Marxist theorists, centrally including Althusser (1970/2014) and Gramsci (1929–1935/1971), also argued for the primacy of ideology and values to social stability. Ideology in the Marxist tradition tends to be viewed more narrowly and negatively than the conception of ethics presented here, but the argument that subjects are interpolated by an ideological matrix that legitimizes and perpetuates status quo sociopolitical relations converges substantially with the argument at hand.

The ideas of Althusser, Gramsci, and Weber gained enduring notoriety, but have often been ignored by more contemporary social, political, and economic theorists. Material and structural factors are often studied and explicated with little attention to ideology and ethics (Haidt, 2012; Hutchinson, 2012; Pulcini, 2013). This neglect is particularly clear in the modern study of economics, which proceeds as if monetary transactions constitute a neutral means of exchange instead of a projection of sociopolitical relations, values, aspirations, and so on (Streeck, 2017).

Recent decades have witnessed renewed interest in ethics, subjectivity, and politics. Haidt (2012), for example, claims that sociopolitical and economic behavior is centrally driven by deeply held, and not necessarily conscious values. He explains that individuals "bind themselves into political teams that share moral narratives" (p. xxiii) and conduct themselves accordingly. Even when individuals believe they are making logical, reasoned decisions, they actually tend to reason backward to justify intuitive or emotional conclusions. For example, one may consciously believe that one's choice of presidential candidate has nothing to do with the candidate's race or gender, yet actually be motivated by unconscious bias. Streeck (2017) argues that "dreams, promises, and imagined satisfaction" (p. 210) prove central to even the seeming materiality of economic behavior, while Cushman (1995) claims that cultural understandings of self and other, right and wrong, often decisively frame political struggle. The secret of effective politicians and social activists alike, according to Cushman, lies in presenting their constituents with a narrative resonant with their ethical compass. He writes, "Attempts at political change are only effective when activists put forth a moral framework that is capable of guiding the population in determining what is good and proper" (1995, p. 351). Successful politicians and activists must speak to immediate, material circumstances, certainly; in order to instantiate a paradigm shift, however, they must transcend particular issues. They must activate fundamental ethical questions. As Critchley (2007) explains, "Political action does not flow from the cunning of reason, some materialist or idealist philosophy of history, or socio-economic determinism, but rather from . . . ethical experience" (p. 92)—from the embodied, motivating perception of justice and injustice, suffering and its relief. A public must have a basic shared understanding of reality, goals for the future, and how to achieve them in order to effectively engage in grassroots political activity (The Free Association, 2011; Streeck, 2017).

The idea that ethical precepts lie at the heart of political activity and social change is increasingly borne out by scientific research. Terms like "emotional culture," "emotional framing," and "emotional harnessing" proliferate in contemporary social and political theory, which increasingly suggests that personal and cultural ethical attitudes—largely subliminal and expressed through feelings—strongly influence political sentiments and behavior (Ruiz-Junco, 2013).

If ethics do in fact lie at the heart of sociopolitical relations, this would explain the notoriously troublesome finding that self-interest is a poor predictor of policy preferences—the recalcitrance of political opinion in the face of overwhelming data (Geffner, 2006). Contradiction between self-interest and actual decisions is of course familiar to analytic clinicians, who observe in intimate detail the ways ethical values and fundamental narratives about self, other, and world powerfully impact behavior—and resist change.

Haidt (2012) suggests that the obstinate and often self-defeating nature of ethical mores may trace evolutionary advantage. He hypothesizes that ethics might have allowed our ancestors to transcend self-interest and devote themselves to collective ventures. Shared axiology is essential to binding people into groups that can accomplish large-scale, time-consuming projects. In a study of origins of religion, Berman (2000) makes a similar claim: religious doctrine facilitated the solidarity required for modern civilization. Thus, ethics may be located at the heart of politics in two senses: first, as central to participation in collective life, and second, as central to the formation of collective life itself.

From one perspective, the primacy of ethics to social change paints a moving, humanistic picture. Ethical principles animate behavior. Deeply-held values supersede petty concerns. When it comes down to it, passion drives decision-making. Political transformation ultimately depends on connecting with people's hearts and values (Sennett, 1998). Viewed differently, this idea becomes disturbing. Modern rulers, having grasped the imperative of psychological and moral validity, now merely manipulate public sentiment. "Manufactured consent" replaces force in maintaining the prevailing hegemony (Gramsci, 1971; Herman & Chomsky, 1988). Modern media technologies render this manipulation alarmingly facile, especially in the current digital era (Taplin, 2017).

In this context, the path to subversive social change lies through cultivation of a collective ethical subjectivity capable of defying the status quo. That is, subversive social and political evolution in our contemporary landscape requires subjects who can observe and disrupt the structural and strategic process through which they are conditioned. An immense amount of effort and resource goes into manipulating subjective experience—what we think we want, who we think our enemies are, and so on is increasingly engineered in the service of a powerful elite—and into the active suppression of both critical and expansive, free-associative thinking. A thoughtless, conformist subjectivity is only reinforced by an economy of human attention, personality marketing, and so on. Resisting this process becomes paramount to radical social change.

DISRUPTIVE ETHICAL ENGAGEMENT

In keeping with the above project of resistance, subversive phenomena must disruptively engage dynamic, embodied philosophical understandings of human nature and human good. This, of course, proves challenging. Shaped by a bricolage of cultural and familial heritages, life events, disposition, media programming, and so on, ethics powerfully influence behavior, often in the absence of conscious reflection. At once personal and cultural, at times firmly avowed, at times latent, ethical values infamously resist change—particularly via rational logic. That said, ethics do in fact shift. Pathways range from media propaganda to focused conversations with neighbors and friends. Subversive ethical disruption must be distinguished from a more manipulative strategy.

Subversive processes unfold from within a given system, in dialogue with the would-be subverted entity. They generate provocative discourse, but do not impose answers. As in any true conversation, the endpoint of a subversive process eludes prediction. Subversion leads toward the creative unknown. Its essence lies in the process—the messy, destabilizing process—of disturbing homeostasis, not in a particular outcome. This does not mean that subversive phenomena lack their own ethical compass or ideology. Quite the opposite. However, the key to subversion lies in opening space for new, unpredictable developments, not in enforcing predetermined values.

This distinguishes subversively disruptive ethical engagement from ideological manipulation and manufactured consent. Such manipulation is not a dialogue, but a sinister hypnosis. It's an imposition—insidious, certainly, but top-down. Furthermore, it doesn't actually alter the established paradigm; rather, ideological manipulation serves precisely to maintain the status quo (Chomsky, 2014; Foucault, 1975). It is arguably the glue that holds the late capitalist machine together (Althusser, 1970/2014; Gramsci, 1929–1935/1971). Thus, the effectiveness of media campaigns and other strategies employed by those in power to manipulate the ethical sensibilities of the public cannot be understood as subversive.

The dialogic, open-ended nature of subversion also distinguishes it from dogmatic factions, such as ISIS which, unlike the manipulative reproduction of prevailing ideology described above, often do disrupt prevailing sociopolitical relations. However, such dogmatic ideology imposes a particular, foregone agenda. Contra the dialogic nature of subversive forces, dogmatic factions definitionally impart rigid, predetermined ideology.

If not through force, fear, or manipulation, how might subversive ethical engagement proceed? Haidt (2012) presents an extensive, empirically-grounded analysis of what I would call subversively disruptive ethical engagement that highlights salient features and facilitative factors. To begin with, simply thinking in a critical and open-minded fashion about ethical themes potentiates subversion of a prevailing ethos. Critically questioning existing beliefs and behavior, engaging challenging topics from multiple perspectives, and exploring alternative ways of being disrupts the perpetuation of the status quo. Conceptualizing inspiring and viable alternatives also proves key to individuals and groups earnestly questioning existing ideals and practices. A sense of possibility, one might say, is vital to subversion (Haidt, 2012). Subversive ethical reflection demands an attitude at once deconstructive and imaginative.

This sort of thinking demands honesty and effort. Questioning core ethical precepts and behavior provokes uncomfortable feelings. Doubt about basic existential concerns can feel destabilizing, threatening one's modus operandi and potentially jeopardizing intimate relationships, job satisfaction, internal cohesion, and so on. Haidt (2012) thus discusses various facilitative factors, including explicitly valuing this kind of thinking. Character traits such as honesty, curiosity, and openmindedness also prove conducive to subversive ethical engagement, as does ample time and space for reflection. In contrast, situations of excessive pressure foreclose the process. When individuals feel stressed, overwhelmed, or threatened, thinking in flexible, creative, and curious ways becomes more challenging. Indeed, when overly pressured, people tend to cling more tightly to previously held beliefs (Haidt, 2012).[3] Thus, subversive ethical reflection demands a certain kind of freedom.

Interpersonal relationships also play an important role in subversive ethical reflection. Nonmanipulative ethical change tends to occur through focused conversations with trusted others, especially across differences (Haidt, 2012). This makes sense, considering the inherently interpersonal nature of ethics, and the importance of intimate relationships in addressing difficult emotional and psychological tasks. Simply attempting to explain things from one's own perspective facilitates earnest ethical reflection, as does contact with differing views—simply living in a diverse community promotes critical ethical reflection (Haidt, 2012). In order for interpersonal dialogue to inspire genuinely disruptive reflection and change, however, individuals must feel emotionally connected. They must share a basic trust, rapport, and respect, experiencing one another as empathic, flexible, and receptive; when individuals feel dismissed or rigidly criticized, they tend to cling to their ideas with increased fanaticism. In other words, a relationship with a high potential for subversive engagement of ethical values contains both closeness and difference, validation and disruption. Such a relationship can be conceived as "optimally marginal."

OPTIMAL MARGINALITY

Subversive phenomena tend to unfold from a position of "optimal marginality" (McLaughlin, 2001), neither too distal nor proximal to the mainstream. Although arising from within a given system, subversive forces also disrupt that system, and thus require meaningful difference. Subversion demands contact, but also distance. This position of proximity and remoteness, withinness and withoutness can be thought of as "optimally marginal": a particular sort of marginality, that carries particular advantages. Optimal marginality involves a balance between intimacy and periphery, deconstruction and affirmation, that precludes the self-absorption, nihilism, and destructiveness of many radical movements (Corbett, 2001). Subversive factions simultaneously face in—cultivating space to reflect, process, dream, and live apart from the pressures of existing sociopolitical relations—and face out, courageously confronting the established order and participating in the extant community (The Free Association, 2011).

The key to optimal marginality lies in a particular sort of engagement with the mainstream. Optimally marginal discourse offers trenchant critique in intelligible terms. It has "access to the creative core of an intellectual tradition, without being bound by institutional restrictions" (McLaughlin, 2001, as cited in Bos et al., 2005, p. 208). It often anticipates sociocultural and political changes. The subversive hero is a rebel, but one with charismatic appeal. He capitalizes on his marginality by portraying it in terms of values recognizable and palatable to the mainstream (e.g., courage, independence, discernment). Her ideas are disruptive, but compelling (Bos et al., 2005). This position saves her from the fate of many oppositional movements: a recapitulation of the hegemony through her own defection (Foucault, 1975). Bos, Park, and Pietikeinen (2005) use Eric Fromm and R. D. Laing to illustrate an optimally marginal position. Both Fromm and Laing were cultural dissidents, yet their messages resonated with broad sociocultural sentiments. Their books were widely read and influenced popular discourse.

The idea of optimal marginality highlights the variability of subversive phenomena. The hegemonic defines the subversive. That is, the ethical vision of a particular sociopolitical status quo determines what might constitute a disruptive, optimally marginal alternative (Bos et al., 2005). This understanding of optimum marginality converges with broader understandings of creativity and change. For example, The Free Association, a group of veteran activist-authors reflecting on their careers, likens the optimal marginality of effective activism to "the finest jazz [which] exists on the edge of unlistenable noise" (The Free Association, 2011, p. 46). Radical creativity deliberately pushes the boundaries of existing standards, providing sufficient resonance with those standards to keep the audience listening, while challenging and changing those same standards at the same time. Similarly, ecologists realize the generative potential of liminal spaces, where life forms are challenged by new and evolving environs without having to forgo the protection of their familiar milieu (Howitt, 2001). This sort of optimal marginality may thus be analogized to a sort of fertile borderland built on a tension between known and unknown, order and chaos, harmony and disintegration.

Nietzsche (1872/1999) discusses such a borderland in *The Birth of Tragedy*, using the ancient Greek Gods Apollo and Dionysus to explicate principles of order and chaos, which exist in optimum tension in creative process. Nietzsche posits chaos and irrationality as essential to the vitality and disruptiveness of true creativity; on the other hand, for creativity to take form, to become intelligible and transcendent, order becomes indispensable. Psychoanalyst Ken Corbett (2001) echoes this sentiment, postulating an essential dialectic between coherence, integration, and mastery, on the one hand, and chaos, disturbance, and possibility on the other. He writes that human development "is infused with an interplay between centrality and marginality" (p. 313), requiring challenge and novelty, but also "the quotidian rhythm of regularity" (p. 330). Also like Nietzsche, Corbett argues that when one side of the centrality-marginality dialectic dominates, problems occur. He illustrates this point with traditional conservative over-reliance on stability and conformity, on one hand, and postmodern liberal hyperbolic deconstruction and relativism on the other. The former results in authoritarian rigidity and stigmatization of difference, the latter in chaos, self-absorption, and anomie.

Optimal ethical development can be conceptualized in similar terms: overemphasis on collectivity and order leads to a loss of individual moral agency (Arendt, 1963), while overemphasis on individuality and nonconformity to a lack of moral coherence (MacIntyre, 1981). The former manifests in mindless fulfilment of social roles and duties, no matter how morally reprehensible (Arendt, 1963) and in a loss of individuality central to phenomena like suicide bombing (Volkan, 2014). The latter manifests in a withdrawal from participation in collective political and civic life (Putnam, 2000), an impoverishment of collective ethical discourse (MacIntyre, 1981; Sandel, 1982), and a subjective sense of alienation and emptiness (Cushman, 1995; Durkheim, 1897/1951).

Although a measure of success inheres in the concept of optimum marginality, anxiety also accompanies marginality, optimal and otherwise. Setting oneself apart (or being set apart) from the mainstream involves risk. As inherently precarious, marginality breeds anxiety. Tolerating such anxiety over time is difficult, but essential to sustaining an effective marginality. Bos et al. (2005) consequently position solidarity as indispensable to optimal marginality, and hence to subversive social change. This accords with broader ideas about the importance of solidarity to successful social movements (The Free Association, 2011; Pulcini, 2013).

SOLIDARITY AND ARTICULATION OF A COMPELLING ETHICAL VISION

Precarity adheres in a subversive position: optimal marginality entails constant risk of both cooption and dissolution. Because subversive forces threaten the established order, they face continual attack (Bos et al., 2005; Corbett, 2001). Any organization, individual, or philosophy occupying a subversive, optimally marginal position, then, must withstand this attack, and withstand it over time. This involves surviving efforts at eradication as well as the pressure to capitulate and conform. Doing so appears to demand solidarity among the subversive faction and, relatedly, clarity of ethical vision (Bos et al., 2005; The Free Association, 2011; Pulcini, 2013).

A felt sense of solidarity mitigates the anxiety generated by a marginal position. Dwelling in the fertile but precarious borderland between civilization and its discontents requires camaraderie. The would-be saboteur must feel connected to others in order to persist at length. Effective social and political movements tend to maintain a considerable measure of internal cohesion, while failed movements frequently devolve through divisiveness. Effective movements also attract new and diverse support, building relationships of solidarity within broader society (The Free Association, 2011; McMillan & Chavis, 1986; Pulcini, 2013). This has been well recognized by government and business elites, who seek strategically to dissemble popular solidarity. This has been particularly true in the United States following the subversive period of the 1960s and early 1970s (Chomsky, 2014). In order to cultivate and sustain internal solidarity, in the face of powerful and systemic attacks on linking (Layton, 2006), solidarity must be built on a firm but flexible foundation. Firm, in order to withstand attack and inspire dedication. Flexible, in order to adapt and endure over time, avoiding dogmatism and cooption. Ethics, in the Platonic-Aristotelian understanding, offers precisely such a platform.

A coherent, compelling ethical vision plays an important role in processes of subversive social change on multiple counts. First, as just noted, ethics provide a supple basis for solidarity. Successful social movements tend to transcend specific issues to engage fundamental ethical themes; they do not simply criticize the established order, but rather offer a positive alternative vision. They offer something to rally around not merely to rally against. A positive ethical vision inspires commitment over time and attracts allies to the would-be subversive movement (Gramsci, cited in Cushman, 2005, p. 412). In contrast to dogma, which can also serve as a powerful basis for group solidarity, ethics affords a flexible basis for cohesion. Because ethics are inherently nonprescriptive, they allow for adaptation, evolution, and variability.

Additionally, if ethics are indeed central to sociopolitical relations, then articulation of a compelling ethical vision is important to a strategy of optimal marginality. That is, optimal marginality vis-à-vis sociopolitical relations involves articulating an ethical vision at once disruptive to and conversant with mainstream ethical philosophy. Subversion of the established order involves entering hegemonic ethical discourse in an optimally marginal way: one that presents a compelling but critical ethical vision, at once resonant and disruptive. Such a vision questions prevailing principles but shares enough conceptual overlap to facilitate dialogue (Bos et al., 2005).

Finally, a compelling and viable alternative ethical vision appears important to willingness to relinquish the status quo. As discussed, in order to surrender deeply-held beliefs and modify habitual ways of being, individuals must be presented with animating substitutes. Ethics bind individuals to particular stories, particular communities—to the world. Absent an alternative, it can prove impossibly hard to let go (The Free Association, 2011; Haidt, 2012; Heidegger, 1927/1962).

CONCLUSION

Subversive processes disrupt prevailing status quos, unfolding from within a given system, and disturbing that system at its foundation. Subversion is typically considered in the context of sociopolitical relations, the complex and historically specific nature of which renders the subversive elusive and variable. In a sense, what is subversive can only be determined post hoc. Yet subversive phenomena also share certain features. Subversion can be thought about abstractly, in terms of intrinsic qualities, and also concretely, in terms of actual impact.

Specifically, disruption of the status quo through a disturbance of a given system's fundamental ethos appears essential or intrinsic to subversion—part of an ontology of subversive phenomena so to speak. Meanwhile, optimal marginality, solidarity, and the articulation and dissemination of a compelling alternative ethical vision can be seen as secondary or auxiliary to subversion. These features play a supportive role in subversive processes, helping translate subversive impetus into political achievement. This distinction between intrinsic and auxiliary features may help illuminate the gap, noted previously, between psychoanalysis's seeming subversiveness and its material traction.

NOTES

1. In defining *subversion* I have made use of the following sources: *Dictionary.com* unabridged, "Subvert," http://www.dictionary.com/browse/subvert; *The Free Dictionary.com*, "Subvert," http://thefredictionary.com/subvert; *Merriam-Webster.com*, "Subvert," https://www.merriam-webster.com/dictionary/subvert.
2. Ideology has a more abstract, disembodied, conscious, rigid, and negative connotation than ethics. Ideology exists solely in mind, while ethics involve subconscious and embodied dimensions. Ideology is often prescriptive, dogmatically applied regardless of circumstance.
3. This is why crises, from breaking up with a partner to experiencing a natural disaster, which tend to evoke ethical questions, often lead to an entrenchment of previously held positions or a blind adoption of dogma, rather than to the ethical reflexivity described here. Because crises create situations of pressure and precariousness, they often fail to afford the time, space, flexibility, support, and safety that Haidt (2012) finds crucial to authentic ethical reappraisal.

Chapter Two

Psychoanalysis as a Subversive Phenomenon

Psychoanalysis is both a theory and a practice—or rather, many theories and many practices—as well as an historical phenomenon. In the United States, where analytic training required a medical degree for decades, clinical and academic psychoanalysis evolved in distinct directions: the valuable critical function of academic psychoanalysis remained largely confined to humanities departments, while applied psychoanalysis retreated from social theory and broad ethical discourse (Lear, 1998; Zaretsky, 2015). Defining psychoanalysis can feel like an impossible task.

This is a book about psychoanalysis at a metalevel: it is a theoretical endeavor that examines psychoanalysis abstractly. Yet I am primarily a clinician, trained in clinical programs, and wary of divisions between practice and theory. Also, I do not think psychoanalysis can be meaningfully conceptualized as subversive or otherwise without including its primary identificatory practice in the calculation. Thus, I strive to hold both theoretical and applied psychoanalysis in mind throughout this project.

Fierce debate surrounds psychoanalysis's basic ontology. In its sweeping curiosity about human experience, essential skepticism, and concern with eternal, existential themes, psychoanalysis can readily be cast as philosophy (Lear, 1998; Tauber, 2010, 2012; Thompson; 1995). On the other hand, in its creativity, unpredictability, and receptivity to the unconscious, psychoanalysis can be conceptualized as art (Bollas, 1999; Bromberg, 1998). Regard for the unconscious leads some theorists to categorize psychoanalysis as a fundamentally spiritual or mystical discipline, requiring faith in the unknown and contacting the deepest reaches of the psyche (e.g., Bettelheim, 1983; Eigen, 2001, 2011; Fromm, 1950). In keeping with Freud's original conception, psychoanalysis can also be thought of as a science, exemplifying the rigorous and open-minded inquiry that define a scientific outlook at its best (Racker, 1966; Wallwork, 1991), and resting on a medico-scientific evidentiary basis (Shedler, 2010; Wachtel, 2010; Westen et al., 2004). Relevant to this project, psychoanalysis can also be classified as a form of social critique. Analytic theory traces the potent, bidirectional influence of psyche and culture, frequently indicting the established order in psychopathology (Aron & Starr, 2013; Danto, 2005; Jacoby, 1983; Zaretsky, 2015). Alternatively, psychoanalysis can be thought of as transdisciplinary (Gentile & Macron, 2016), or simply uncategorizable (Aron & Starr, 2013).

I believe our ways of conceptualizing the epistemological and ontological foundations of psychoanalysis matter greatly, but my purpose here is simply to provide a cohesive conception of psychoanalysis in order to explore its subversive features. Without negating additional classifications, I propose that psychoanalysis can be compelling cast as a discipline of character—as an ethic, in the Platonic-Aristotelian sense of the term. Not only do I believe this categorization of psychoanalysis makes sense intrinsically, but psychoanalysis *being* an ethic, ontologically, is in fact key to its subversive functioning. In order to converse subversively with any particular hegemonic ethos, psychoanalysis must embody an ethos per se.

PSYCHOANALYSIS AS AN ETHIC

At first glance, psychoanalysis and ethics may seem odd bedfellows. Freud (e.g., 1930/1961) sharply criticized conventional morality, implicating its repressive grip in psychopathology, and pathologizing the human drive toward religion. Freud is pointedly clear that if we try too hard to be good—if we try to get rid of unwanted aspects of ourselves and others through incessantly policing—our so-called bad parts only gain traction. Clinical psychoanalysis thus aspires toward a space free from judgment in which thoughts, feelings, fantasies, and histories can be fully explored. Analytic neutrality involves receptivity to all the patient brings. With any luck, patients adopt this receptive stance, loosening the grip of internalized norms and social mores. Further, analytic therapists seek to nurture patients' autonomy, refraining from offering directives, or imposing standards—including their own moral values. These fundamental commitments to neutrality and autonomy have fostered caution when it comes to asserting ethical claims (Cushman, 1995; Wallwork, 1991). Even the recent "ethical turn" within psychoanalysis concentrates on the relationship between therapist and client, centrally including the ethical obligation of therapist toward patient (see, for example, Goodman & Severson, 2016), rather than advancing a critical social vision.

Antipathy between psychoanalysis and morality hinges on a deontological conception of ethics, however—it involves rejection of prescriptive guidelines of comportment, especially when followed through guilt, fear, or groupthink. As Wallwork (1991) states, if ethics involve "preaching or telling others in some direct, caustic way how to act" (p. 2), then psychoanalysis staunchly resists them. By contrast, if ethics are approached from a Platonic-Aristotelian perspective, psychoanalysis can be considered an ethical praxis par excellence.

Platonic-Aristotelian ethics indicate a basic conception of human flourishing, or "eudaimonia." This includes theories of human nature, human excellence, and human good (Harcourt, 2013). Such theories cannot be separated from lived experience, but are rather embodied, flexible, and often unarticulated. The vicissitudes of familial and cultural influence, life experiences, and the like shape each individual's ethical development. That said, virtue ethics suggest that ethical conduct is ultimately a personal responsibility, and thus encourages deliberate involvement with ethical themes. The examined life is the one worth living: the idiosyncratic and ongoing process of character development is foundational to eudaimonia. Such character development happens through consistent and candid self-reflection, the mundane tasks of life, and interpersonal relationships, particularly those of close proximity. Parents centrally impact a child's ethical development, while adults hone ethics through friendship (Aristotle, trans. 2002).

Indeed, though highly personal, virtues only make sense in the context of relationships. They are definitionally concerned with how to treat others (MacIntyre, 1981). The presence of the other forms the foundation of ethical inquiry, and all answers to the eternal conundrum of eudaimonia bear political implications. Critical, sustained self-reflection leads directly to the question of how to treat others, and to that of how to build a society that supports collective flourishing.

In circular fashion, a social milieu that supports flourishing is in turn foundational to ethics (Aristotle, trans. 2002). Character development occurs in an inherently interpersonal world, and in the absence of good-enough relationships (especially parental relationships early on), it flounders. Even in the presence of adequate parenting and education, however, ethical sensibilities represent a rather confused bundle of likes and dislikes, prejudices, life experiences, etc.—unless we make a concerted effort otherwise. Aristotle (trans. 2002) thus prescribes persistent, critical ethical reflection, and an ongoing endeavor to align ourselves with evolving conclusions.

This is no mean feat. In contrast to sanguine contemporary notions of thinking positive and being mindful, Aristotelian character development is painful. It involves disillusionment, humility, and reconciliation. Critical self-reflection entails confronting flaws and relinquishing treasured self-conceptions. It also involves integrating myriad aspects of the self. Aristotle (trans. 2002) saw virtues as a combination of rational, emotional, and social capacities, flexibly deployed in response to infinitely variable circumstances. Morality must be integrated with appetites and passions, and there is no substitute for sound judgment.

Despite its arduousness, virtuous conduct should be pursued as an end in itself, rather than for ulterior purposes. According to Aristotle (trans. 2002), virtues should be honed deliberately, with pride, and even pleasure. While virtue ethics have been critiqued as self-centered and ineffectual vis-à-vis broader discourse (e.g., Louden, 1989; Nussbaum, 1999), theorists in this tradition emphasize the importance of the intrinsic motivation to collective ethics and flourishing (e.g., Aristotle, trans. 2002; MacIntyre, 1981). As Aristotle (trans. 2002) observed, laws incommensurate with personal beliefs are only as strong as the threat of punishment; thus, the characters, motivations, and aspirations of individual members of society are crucial to the whole.

Psychoanalysis overlaps substantially with this interpretation of ethics. To begin with, psychoanalysis and virtue ethics share the same basic line of inquiry: like virtue ethicists, analytic theorists and therapists are interested in the nature of and relationship between human nature, human excellence, and human good (Harcourt, 2013; Lear, 1998). Analysts and virtue ethicists engage similar questions, such as the extent of conscious reason, the relationship between reason and passion, the nature of freedom, and the responsibility we have toward the one another. Like virtue ethicists, moreover, analytic therapists understand that the question of how to live cannot be fully answered in theoretical or abstract terms. It is a question woven into the fabric of daily life. Its answer is deeply personal, and continually evolving. Wisdom about human flourishing may require deliberation, but can never be cleaved from phenomenology. Ethics, therefore, cannot be prescriptively applied. Because of the idiosyncratic, embodied, and situational nature of ethics, neither the Socratic philosopher nor the analytic therapist offers concrete answers. Each instead adopts an attitude of skepticism, receptivity, and regard for difference and autonomy (Thompson, 2004).

Yet such an attitude itself constitutes an ethical position. While analytic practitioners do not pronounce ethical dictums, this does not make analysis value-free. By offering constructions of health and sanity, suffering and healing, psychoanalysis upholds an ethical vision (Cushman, 1995). As Carnochan (2001) writes, “Psychoanalysis, as a therapeutic endeavor, an endeavor that seeks to redeem us from suffering, is intrinsically a theory of virtue” (p. 293). Thompson (2004) agrees, noting that like virtue ethics,

> Psychoanalysis is both a collection of ideas and a method based upon those ideas whose goal is the right way to live . . . psychoanalysis is an “ethic” in

> the sense that it concerns the manner by which individuals conduct themselves. (p. 1)

In other words, analytic theory expresses ethical ideas. Many of these ideas, moreover, converge with Aristotle's conclusions about character development.

Both analytic theory and virtue ethics position deliberation and character development as vital to human flourishing. Both maintain that ethical sensibilities powerfully impact perception of self, others, and environment, and therefore behavior (Harcourt, 2013). Absent concerted deliberation, moreover, ethics reflect nebulous and often contradictory influences and particular life experiences, largely outside of conscious awareness. We are all inevitably caught up in what Layton (2015) calls "normative unconscious processes." This makes it incumbent upon individuals (and societies) to submit ourselves to close examination, in a critical, spacious, ongoing way. Psychoanalytic and Aristotelian ethics alike involve "interrupting the motions of normative life and calling into question the ways that one's subjectivity, practices, and commitments uphold the status quo" (Goodman & Severson, 2016, p. 7). This is difficult, painful, and ongoing.

We cannot simply decide to be a certain way and, voilà, become transformed. Rather, we must work patiently with ourselves as we are, in the context of evolving ideas about how we want to be; parts of the self cannot be buried nor denied, but instead require integration and balance. Freud's tripartite model of id, ego, and superego resembles the Platonic-Aristotelian appetite, spirit, and reason and despite privileging the ego/reason, both models warn against repression (Lear, 1998).

From both a psychoanalytic and virtue ethics perspective, moreover, character development occurs axiomatically through relationships. Ethics arise through and in response to our relationships with other people. This is true both existentially and developmentally—Aristotle and Freud both indict inadequate parenting and general childhood socialization in faulty ethical development (Harcourt, 2013). Each was nonplussed with the predominant social and moral education of their time, and Freud's disdain for the latter has led to the widespread misperception that he opposed morals, period. In fact, by doubting the credentials of morality and of the superego, Freud did not mean we should dispense with either (Harcourt, 2013; Zaretsky, 2015). Freud recognized the need for ethical development but proposed a more Aristotelian path to its pursuit. Like Aristotle, Freud believed virtues should be followed through freely chosen commitment, in light of their intrinsic worth (Wallwork, 1991). Ethics enforced through fear or rigid social norms, or followed through complacent habit, are spurious in both Aristotelian and Freudian paradigms, regardless of outcome. Ethical conduct pursued through the tyranny of the superego is no better than that pursued through fear of the police: freedom is crucial to ethics in both views.

And yet, freedom in both traditions is also circumscribed. Ethical reflection and the psychic freedom it affords cannot be extricated from society and politics—beginning, again, with interpersonal relationships. Because ethical development relies on (or fails through) other people, Aristotle prescribes friendship, and Freud therapy. Each of these types of relationships teaches and challenges, while also respecting autonomy. Each serves a pedagogic function, but without direct intervention, and involves care, candor, and dialogue. Both friendship and therapy also embody and foster certain ethical values. Analytic therapy, for example, can be conceptualized as a relationship that models "a way of being that is honest, self-reflective, critical, humble, curious, compassionate, and respectful of and willing to learn from difference" (Cushman, 2015, p. 424).

This convergence between psychoanalysis and virtue ethics suggests that the former fundamentally engages ethics in the Platonic-Aristotelian sense of the term. This makes psychoanalysis well poised to participate in the ethical discourse and development that upholds and modifies established sociopolitical relations. Whether psychoanalysis engages ethics in specifically subversive manner, and whether analytic ethical values might operate subversively in contemporary culture remains to be seen.

DISRUPTION OF THE STATUS QUO

The sine qua non of subversion is disruption or serious alteration of a particular status quo. Many authors have elaborated the disruptive function of analytic theory and practice vis-à-vis existing norms and habitual ways of being, including Freud's originary disturbance of reigning Victorian ideology (e.g., Aron & Starr, 2013; Bollas, 2007; Lear, 1998; Marcuse, 1955; Moss, 2018; Thompson, 1995; Zaretsky, 2015). Indeed, so much has been written about psychoanalysis's capacity to disturb the prevailing status quo that at least three distinct paradigms can be traced: 1) deconstruction of processes of internalization and reification of the social order, 2) liberation of unconscious and libidinal forces, and 3) illumination of liminality, paradox, and complexity. These paradigms are not necessarily exhaustive—nor mutually exclusive.

Deconstructive Paradigm

Psychoanalysis illustrates the influence of social and cultural mores on our ethics and aspirations, including our most private thoughts, feelings, and desires. Freud (1930/1961) exposed the imprint of the social in the most intimate recesses of human development—and showed that absent reflection, we tend to adopt this imprinting as authentic and true. Analytic praxis disrupts this process, introducing a pause in the smooth propagation of the status quo. Psychoanalysis affords the opportunity to witness social reproduction, considering which aspects of the social order we might wish to keep, and which we might wish to discard or transform. We have a chance to wonder where our desires, hatreds, and aspirations come from, and to imagine alternatives. The freedom of free association in this view involves loosening the strictures of habitual, socially-conditioned thoughts. Analytic deconstruction involves treating the familiar with curiosity and skepticism; assumed facts become problematized; truth and desire are revealed as mutable, and socially mediated (Fanon, 1961/2004; Wallwork, 1991). This undermines the individual superego, as well as the broader social status quo of which it is an accomplice.

This means that psychoanalytic theory and therapy contradict the cynical inevitability and relativism of certain strands of postmodernism and leftist politics (Cushman, 2005). While no one can escape the internalization of social norms—which is in fact integral to civilization—psychoanalysis holds that individuals can shape the process. We can talk back. We are profoundly shaped but not imprisoned by fate. Through reflection and effort, we can assume a role of increased authorship in our thoughts, desires, and lives (Cushman, 2005; Fong, 2012; Summers, 2013; Wallwork, 1991). In a sense, analytic therapy teaches patients to think. This deconstructive thinking and spirit of agency opposes the sociopolitical status quo and its repetitive abrogation of alternatives. Now more than ever in the world of data-driven manipulation of subjectivity, analytic deconstruction becomes vital to projects of resistance.

Antinomian Paradigm

Psychoanalysis's capacity to subvert the status quo can also be understood from an "antinomian" perspective (Cohan & Jenkins, 2016). The word "antinomian" comes from the Greek word for lawlessness, and emphasizes the disruptive nature of unconscious psychic processes. Analytic theory holds that there are dimensions of human experience that transcend our capacity to perceive, much less rationally comprehend, and that illuminating these dimensions disrupts order, period. By attending to unconscious processes, analytic practice may undermine the norms, logic, and systematization upon sociopolitical orders depend (Lear, 1998; Marcuse, 1955). By elaborating unconscious desire, analytic practice births something unpredictable, dissensual, and potentially subversive—antiauthoritarian par excellence[1] (Critchley, 2007; Lacan 1992/1986).

The aim of psychoanalysis in this view is to uncover and articulate authentic and often unconscious desire, dismantling habitual defenses and false ambitions along the way (Lacan 1992/1986). Analytic therapy affords an outlet for the Dionysian aspect of psyche: passionate, sensual, sexual, wild, creative, and frequently destructive. It connects us to the never fully manipulatable libidinal lifeforce rooted in our bodies, nurturing an idiosyncratic creativity that cannot be manufactured (Bollas, 1999; Marcuse, 1955). This thwarts efforts to contrive desire and coopt creativity.

While both the antinomian and deconstructive traditions celebrate psychoanalysis's disruption of automatic processes of internalization and reification of social mores, helping patients articulate their unique emotional truths with increasing clarity, they differ in their approach to enduring freedom from social strictures. In the deconstructive view, deliberate self-reflection and activity in keeping with one's ethical compass allows a person to increasingly become the source of their own freedom (Wallwork, 1991). This is not a theory of omnipotent control, but it does suggest that the arduous and deliberate process of character development allows us to have greater agency in our own lives, and thus greater capacity to disrupt the status quo. It echoes Freud's claim that, "Analysis . . . set[s] out . . . to give the patient's ego freedom to decide one way or the other" (as cited in Wallwork, 1991, p. 49).

In contrast, in the antinomian perspective, freedom lies beyond the reach of any rational project. The aim of psychoanalysis is to free patients from themselves, including the deconstructive project of autonomous ethical development. Psychoanalysis's bedrock of free association involves letting go of our conscious, controlling ego, in order to experience a deeper freedom. Freedom comes through fidelity to thoughts, feelings, images, and desires, without attempting to control them. As Thompson (2004) writes, "The words uttered in psychoanalysis *are determined by one's freedom*, if one understands freedom as that which cannot be dictated" (p. 30, emphasis in original). In this view, it is this freedom that opposes the social order, this libidinal energy that animates a subversive subjectivity.

Complexity Paradigm

Analytic theory suggests that truths are dialectical, meanings ambiguous, and people contradictory. The analyst thus adopts an attitude of skepticism, asking patients to contend with uncertainty (Thompson, 2004). Psychoanalysis encourages fluid, paradoxical thought, subverting categories, dichotomies, and moral prescriptions, and making room for previously excluded or pathologized individuals, modes of expression, aspects of the self, and so on (Aron & Starr, 2013; Cushman, 2005; Summers, 2013). Analytic theory substitutes both-and for either-or. It is a theory of multiplicity. The expansive contradictory Freudian cannon reflects the vast complexity of human ontology.

This analytic complexity opposes the presumptions and crystallizing structures upon which the social order depends. Maintenance of status quo sociopolitical relations requires automatic, simplistic, categorical thought. It necessitates heuristics and assumptions that inevitably marginalize certain dimensions of experience and ways of being (Lear, 1998). By giving voice to the gamut of human experience, championing the divergent and inchoate, psychoanalysis works against the status quo. It upholds a subjectivity too vast and fluid to be subjugated.

Taken together, these three paradigms suggest considerable subversive potential—at least in abstract terms. Whether or not psychoanalysis actually functions disruptively vis-à-vis the present sociopolitical status quo is of course a more complicated question.

DISRUPTIVE ETHICAL ENGAGEMENT

Psychoanalysis fundamentally engages ethics and disrupts the habitual or status quo from multiple angles. To function subversively, psychoanalysis would need to disrupt prevailing ethical values and habits, and do so in a particular fashion. Subversive ethical engagement involves critical reflection on deeply held beliefs and values and exploration of alternative ways of being. In contrast to the manipulative variety, subversive ethical engagement respects the autonomy of individual actors, posing questions and instigating dialogue, rather than dictating solutions. Subversive disruption of ethical principles unfolds subtly and unpredictably from within a given system, often from a position of optimal marginality.

In keeping with this theory, psychoanalysis invites critical, creative reflection on ethical themes, pondering difficult questions such as the nature of motivation, the minimum necessary conditions for healthy childhood development, and the limits of freedom and culpability. Analytic treatment offers a protected space in which patients are challenged to examine themselves in their full vicissitudes (Ogden, 2001, 2004; Thompson, 2004). Analytic practice also emphasizes potentiality, seeing patients not only as they are but as they might be, and encouraging the development of alternatives (Summers, 2013; Zepf, 2010). Psychoanalysis is open-ended, privileging autonomy and gradual internally-driven ethical development.

Subversive ethical reflection is difficult and can prove destabilizing, challenging the limits of our capacity to think and feel. Thus, factors that facilitate this kind of engagement are important to consider in an analysis of subversion, especially regarding the translation of intrinsic subversive potential into achieved impact. Such factors include honesty, openmindedness, flexibility, courage, creativity, imagination, freedom, diversity, time, space, conceptualization of a compelling alternative ethical vision, and focused conversations with trusted others (Haidt, 2012). At least in ideal terms,[2] analytic practice embodies many of these attributes.

Honesty, for example, is fundamental to analytic practice. Beyond simply showing up, the patient's most important job is to speak as freely as possible (Thompson, 2004). Clinical psychoanalysis entails a close examination of beliefs, desires, behavior, and so on. It reveals, moreover, that we are predisposed to think the thoughts and endorse the values of our particular social order—clinical psychoanalysis can be thought of as a sort of case study in how radical honesty can disrupt the status quo. This sort of honesty demands flexibility and courage, and psychoanalysis can be seen to foster both, increasing our capacity to tolerate uncomfortable thoughts and feelings and examine issues from multiple views (Lear, 1998; Thompson, 2004; Wallwork, 1991). Analytic theory privileges multiplicity, affirming a picture of human well-being that includes expressing the gamut of thoughts and emotions. Analytic treatment curates respect for the contradictory, paradoxical, and discordant within the self, as well as for differences between patient and analyst (Benjamin, 1988, 1995). Such regard for difference buoys earnest ethical reflection.

Psychoanalysis also supports the autonomy, time, and space that potentiate subversive ethical engagement. Just as emphasis on freedom and self-determination distinguishes subversive from manipulative ethical engagement, so, too, does it differentiate psychoanalysis from formulaic hegemonic approaches to treatment. Psychoanalysis is a long-term and open-ended venture that cannot be forced or rushed (Lear, 1998; Summers, 2013). The analyst's quietude and evenly hovering attention (Freud, 1912/1958d) and invitation to the patient to say whatever comes to mind offers the open space in which sustained ethical reflection can blossom.

In order to depart from a particular paradigm or homeostasis, individuals and societies alike must be able to envision alternatives; they must be able to imagine and experiment with new ideas and ways of being (The Free Association, 2011; Haidt, 2012). Analytic treatment provides a space and relationship conducive to creative exploration. Attention to unconscious processes and belief in the human capacity for change encourages a sense of possibility. Meanwhile, the work of unsticking rigid defense patterns and normative preconceptions frees psychic energy for novel pursuits (Ogden, 2005).

Finally, analytic therapy provides the sort of intimate interpersonal relationship central to ethical development. The Other's presence—their needs, their difference—challenges us to think and adjust our perspective. Ethics arise in response to the suffering Other (Orange, 2009, 2010; Rozmarin, 2007). Analytic therapy cultivates an intimate relationship in which patients can express themselves freely, while also being challenged by the analyst's independent subjectivity, offering a combination of safety and intimacy, risk and difference that aligns with subversive processes.

Thus, on an individual clinical level, psychoanalysis appears to promote subversive ethical engagement. Perhaps historically, psychoanalysis also subverted ethics on a societal level—certainly, Freudian ideas unsettled core Western notions of morality, sexuality, rationality, and so on. More recently, however, psychoanalysis has reified a hegemonic, white, heteronormative ethos. Although analytic precepts in many ways appear countercultural in our contemporary milieu, they are also part and parcel of the established paradigm. I will discuss specific ways in which analytic theory validates and problematizes hegemonic American ethics in the following chapters. Regardless of this ensuing analysis however, in order for psychoanalysis to promote subversive ethical reflection on a sociopolitical scale, significantly greater sociopolitical valence would be required.

Psychoanalysis in the United States today is hypermarginalized. Psychoanalysis became so white, elitist, and out of touch with contemporary sociopolitical and economic issues over the second half of the twentieth century that bringing the outside world into psychoanalysis, rather than the reverse, has been the paramount task. This is a critical and challenging project, but it is not a subversive dialogue with mainstream culture. Subversion of the internal culture of psychoanalysis—making psychoanalysis more relevant across diverse populations—is a precondition to broader subversive impact, but it is not the same thing. Psychoanalysis would need to become more salient in contemporary society, actively engaging the world outside the consulting room in order to function subversively in contemporary culture. Analytic communities would need to build relationships with diverse populations, academic disciplines, and so on, in order to develop the traction requisite to vigorous, potentially subversive ethical engagement with mainstream society.

Encouragingly, from this perspective, a growing consensus within analytic circles views renewed sociopolitical engagement as a task of paramount importance. Analytic theorists and clinicians are increasingly turning attention to sociopolitical and environmental issues and broadening the scope of analytic thinking and practice (see, for example, Akhtar, 2018; Anderson et al., 2011; Altman, 1995; Aron & Starr, 2013; Cushman, 2015; Erlich, 2013; ffytche & Pick, 2016; Fong, 2016; Johanssen, 2019; Layton, 2014, 2015; McGowan, 2016; Moss, 2003, 2016; Oliver, 2004; Orange, 2016; Volkan, 2014; Walls, 2004; Weintrobe, 2013). Often, however, this involves simplistic, reductive application of analytic concepts to social phenomenon, or combining a psychoanalytic understanding of the individual with some other social theory, such as Marxism, rather than a truly social psychoanalysis. Examining contemporary issues such as climate change and racism from an analytic perspective often entails subjectification of structural, political, and economic problems, and a version of identity politics dissociated from broader political and economic context.

In addition to changing the internal culture of psychoanalysis and developing alliances with diverse communities, engaging ethics subversively on a sociopolitical level would involve situating psychoanalysis firmly as an ethical and social discipline, theorizing meaningful links between psyche and society, and articulating an ethical vision for psychoanalysis with sociopolitical implications. A subversive analytic social psychology would illuminate complex, multidirectional processes of psychopathology and psychic enslavement and point toward progressive social change. It would integrate sociohistorical context and political economy and individual subject formation in a full and nuanced way. It would remain rooted in the richly-textured individual subject and offer a uniquely analytic understanding of society. It would help make sense of the contemporary landscape and help imagine alternatives. While contemporary examples of robust analytic social psychology certainly exist (see, for example, Ahktar, 2018; Anderson et al., 2011; ffytche & Pick, 2016; Fong, 2016; Johanssen, 2019; McGowan, 2016) they are uncommon.

AN ETHICAL VISION FOR PSYCHOANALYSIS

A coherent, inspiring, ethical vision appears important to subversive ethical engagement on multiple counts. For individuals and groups alike, having a viable alternative is important to relinquishing entrenched perspectives. Further, a positive ethical vision mitigates the entropy and nihilism that hazard radical political movements; it facilitates internal solidarity and helps a would-be subversive faction attract and sustain support and dedication over time, transcending the confines of particular issues and narrow political battles (Cushman, 2005; The Free Association, 2011; Rorty, 1998). In order to function subversively in a given historical moment, moreover, a particular alternative ethical vision would need to be presented in culturally intelligible terms, in keeping with the concept of optimal marginality. That is, a subversive ethical vision would dialogue with the mainstream, offering both fruitful contact and critical distance.

I believe psychoanalysis contains a compelling ethical vision, which could function as a basis for solidarity within the analytic community, as well as a bridge to broader discourse and political participation. This vision often lies latent, however, undertheorized and articulated within analytic circles, much less within society at large (Cushman, 1995; Harcourt, 2013). Certainly, the recent "ethical turn" in American psychoanalysis has begun an important conversation, but remains largely rooted in the Levinasian tradition of moral responsibility toward the subjective, suffering Other (e.g., Orange, 2009; Rozmarin, 2007). It emphasizes the clinical dyad and its dynamics of doer-done to, injury and reparation, intersubjective vulnerability, moral witnessing, and moral thirdness, as well as a Gadamerican focus on dialogue (e.g., Benjamin, 2004, 2011; Goodman & Severson, 2016; Orange, 2010). It neither consistently engages psychoanalysis as a discipline of character in the Aristotelian paradigm, nor offers an explicit and critical moral vision applied to contemporary society and politics, in the tradition of virtue ethics. Recent writing on psychoanalysis and ethics often discusses the disparate positionalities of therapist and client via the intersubjective ethics of care and recognition but without offering a full ethical critique of the material realities of neoliberal capitalism.

The analytic ethical vision I have in mind would involve a broad philosophical vision of human nature and human flourishing, as well as a suffering and its relief, that points toward political questions and strategies. It would emphasize psychoanalysis as a discipline of character: a process, rooted in a particular relationship, by which we develop our selves. Because these selves are inevitably shaped through normative ethos, analytic character development is essentially critical: it leads directly to analytic social psychology. Part of analytic inquiry into subjective experience involves a Foucauldian desubjectification that reveals structural impingements. Certainly, examples of this kind of ethical thinking within psychoanalysis exist, and I have benefited greatly from them (see, for example, Cushman, 1995, 2015; Layton, 2015, 2016; Thompson, 2004; Summers, 2013; Wallwork, 1991). Still, I believe inhibition of this particular kind of ethical thinking within analytic circles has limited psychoanalysis's capacity to function subversively—across clinical and sociopolitical registers.

Clinically, failure to delineate psychoanalysis's particular ethical vision facilitates inadvertent reification of oppressive social norms. Absent a clear independent ethical vision, analytic practitioners risk upholding normative values (Cushman, 1995). Undertheorization of psychoanalytic ethical precepts at a broad societal level also obscures patients' understanding of the psychoanalytic project, and thus the opportunity to deliberately pursue a disruptive therapeutic modality. It impedes the distinction between psychoanalysis and alternative approaches (Summers, 2013). Culturally, failure to articulate a cogent ethical vision obfuscates psychoanalysis's radical potential, "de-linking" clinical practice and theory from other forms of political resistance. Reluctance to assert ethical positions short circuits potential alliances and forms of engagement, impeding potentially subversive applications of analytic theory (Botticelli, 2004; Cushman, 2005). Again, while renewed interest in ethics and politics is broadly apparent within psychoanalysis, this is a nascent phenomenon, often internally focused, rather than meaningfully linked to a coherent ethical-political project. A truly social and ethical psychoanalysis that integrates historical context and political economy and individual subject formation, rather than simply applying analytic concepts to social phenomenon, or combining a psychoanalytic understanding of the individual with some other social theory remains lacking.

This situation can be traced at least in part to intrinsic qualities of psychoanalysis and psychoanalytic ethics. Psychoanalysis is largely a private, dyadically-focused practice; although analytic clinicians observe a microcosm of political, cultural, and ethical life, linking observations from this register to broader conversations is a fraught and difficult venture, replete with glib and dangerous examples (Volkan, 2014). Further, the ethics of psychoanalysis consists of embodied principles, such as free association, that guide action but which cannot be prescriptively applied. Psychoanalytic ethics are inherently situated: the response of a particular embedded character to the contingencies of their particular life, or the relationship between a particular analytic couple. They stem from close attention to the individual and the dyad—centrally including fidelity to the unpredictable expression of unconscious desire (Critchley, 2007; Lacan, 1992/1986). This means that analytic ethics are inherently dissensual: rooted in the elaboration of the unknown, subjective, and intersubjective, they oppose the broad consensus of status quos. Thus, an abstract ethical vision for psychoanalysis can feel like a contradiction.

And yet the ethics of psychoanalysis, of the contextual, of the subjective, of the related, also aim toward universal truths (Badiou, 2001; Critchley, 2007). The ethics of psychoanalysis consists of what Critchley (2007) calls situated universality, reaching beyond the mundane and idiosyncratic toward the shared and immortal, without ever becoming absolute or prescriptive. Psychoanalytic ethics may be situated, alive, and particular, but also demand deliberation. Prior reflection and commitments condition responsiveness to particular circumstances (Merleau-Ponty, 1945/2012). Cogent abstract ethical principles guide analytic thinking and create the conditions in which the situated ethics of analytic practice emerge.

The ethics of psychoanalysis have also been poorly articulated for reasons beyond the ontology of psychoanalysis and problematic of situated universality. Aspirations toward analytic and scientific neutrality, and neglect of social, political, and ethical issues by clinical psychoanalysis in the middle of the last century, have tended to function as a self-serving professionalism that neglects ethics in general, and risks passively upholding prevailing ethical values and cultural norms in lieu of articulating radical alternatives. Psychoanalysis became a white, elitist profession, eschewing the treatment of marginalized groups and ignoring the ethical issues raised by diverse populations and systemic oppression (Aron & Starr, 2013; Cushman, 1995). Widespread divisiveness within and between analytic communities further undermined the articulation of broad and clear ethical principles (Stepansky, 2009). Enduring ontological and epistemic conundrums have only exacerbated this process (Carnochan, 2001; Mills, 2012). Because psychoanalysis can be understood in many different ways, its philosophical and ethical tenets can appear murky. Psychoanalysis's capacity for conceptualization as a science, a healing practice, a philosophy, a pedagogy, an art, and so on can obscure its existence as an ethical discipline, with accompanying ethical principles.

Regardless of why, psychoanalytic thinkers and clinicians today face the task of articulating analytic ethical principles in intelligible terms, in order to engage in relevant sociopolitical and cultural discourse. And indeed, emerging from a resounding critique of the field's midcentury trajectory, analytic thinkers today increasingly embrace the interpellation of the personal and the political, often engaging ethics along the way (see, for example, Altman, 1995; Cushman, 1995, 2015; Goodman & Severson, 2016; Hollander et al., 2006; Moss, 2016; Orange, 2016; Rozmarin, 2014; Summers, 2013; Volkan, 2014). Fueled by desire to engage in politics and public discourse, revitalize a social analytic understanding of sociopolitical issues, and distinguish psychoanalysis from competing modes of treatment, analytic thinkers appear increasingly willing to make ethical claims.

OPTIMAL MARGINALITY

Subversive processes appear most likely to unfold from a position of optimal marginality, both in dialogue with and opposition to the mainstream. Subversion requires trenchant critique, but also enough relevance and shared language to attract attention and communicate effectively (Bos et al., 2005; The Free Assocation, 2011). Subversion is an embedded, relational process that demands not only dissent but also sufficient connection with the mainstream to engage in genuine dialogue. It disrupts mainstream discourse dialogically, rather than through attack or withdrawal (Bos et al., 2005). Such a strategy guards against reifying power relations through defection (Foucault, 1975) as well as against destructive extremes of deconstruction and purity (Chen, 2017; Rorty, 1998).

Bos et al. (2005) use the early psychoanalytic community to illustrate the concept of effective marginality. At its inception, psychoanalysis engaged in sociocultural, philosophical, and political discourse in ways that both excited widespread interest and challenged hegemonic assumptions. While certainly no stranger to tensions and rivalries, Bos et al. (2005) claim that the early analytic community shared a basic solidarity and enthusiasm that allowed its members to tolerate the anxiety inherent in marginality. Freud in particular typified an optimum marginality, occupying a position of prestige as a white male doctor, yet marginalized on account of his Jewishness and unsettling ideas. Freud possessed enough cachet to understand and articulate important facets of his sociocultural milieu, and enough dystopia for uncompromising critique (Bos et al., 2005). Aron and Starr (2013) corroborate this portrayal of neonate psychoanalysis, highlighting its inherent skepticism, embrace of complexity and paradox, and proclivity for the subterranean, the shadow, the discarded, and oppressed. They note that Freud described psychoanalysis as the "impossible profession," continually opposing cohesion and reification that typically accompany professionalism.

Regardless of why, prewar psychoanalysis did in fact manage to attract considerable attention and to spread quickly, while opposing hegemonic concepts of sexuality, development, mental illness, and the like. Early analysts disturbed existing social norms, but were also part of the broader sociocultural and philosophical movement that has come to be known as postmodernism, constructivism, or deconstructivism (Cushman, 2005). Its central ideas were effectively deployed by a host of revolutionary movements, and were also, simultaneously, changing and being incorporated into mainstream discourse (Zaretsky, 2015).

In postwar America, however, psychoanalysis became ensconced in the hegemonic mental health paradigm. Analysts perpetuated oppressive, pejorative social norms, corroborating an image of psychological health that was white, heteronormative, atomistic, and consumeristic, and downplaying the role of society and ethics in the experience, conceptualization, and treatment of mental illness. More recently, psychoanalysis has become hypermarginalized within the mental health field, as well as within the academy, and society at large (Aron & Starr, 2013; Bos et al., 2005; Zaretsky, 2015). Although analytic thinkers and clinicians increasingly focus on sociopolitical issues, from race and gender to climate change, torture, authoritarianism, and class politics, they do so from a position of suboptimal marginality.

Moving away from historical evidence toward intrinsic qualities of analytic treatment, psychoanalysis can be seen to offer a synthesis of disruption and support, confrontation and validation, resonant with the concept of optimal marginality. On one hand, psychoanalysis disrupts conscious, habitual modus operandi through its particular form of honesty and attention to latent dynamics. It interrupts existing modes of thought and being. On the other hand, as a healing praxis, psychoanalysis seeks to foster psychic equilibrium. It is as much about understanding as it is about not knowing, and clinical practice aspires to put understanding to use in the service of mental health. While psychoanalysis is an arduous, frequently destabilizing venture, mental health involves some degree of acceptance, integration, and stability. Analytic treatment thus provides dependability and validation.

In other words, analysts can be thought of as aspiring toward a sort of optimal marginality, helping patients to feel stable, integrated, and supported, while disrupting their habitual defense mechanisms and patterns of thought. They lean in close enough for patients to feel validated, and out far enough for them to feel challenged. Bromberg (1998) describes this tension as a continual titration of empathy and anxiety gradients. At best, analytic treatment maintains the creative tension between order and chaos, integration and disintegration, knowing and not knowing, coherence and incoherence, Dionysian mess and Apollonian symbolism essential to creativity and change. It offers "a theory of mental freedom that not only allows for the utopian rupture of normativity but also heeds the quotidian rhythm of regularity and the structuring potential of relational reverie" (Corbett, 2001, p. 330). Thus, psychoanalysis can be conceptualized as an optimally marginal embodied practice, despite its suboptimal marginality vis-à-vis contemporary culture. Furthermore, as will be discussed in the ensuing chapters, at level of abstract values, psychoanalysis's ethical vision may present an optimally marginal alternative to the mainstream.

SOLIDARITY

Considerable anxiety inheres in a subversive, optimally marginal position. Subversive phenomena are perpetually at risk of both disintegration and cooption, not to mention hostile persecution. Political resistance is an arduous, often violent endeavor. Tolerating the precarity of marginality and resisting dissolution and assimilation demands an internal sense of solidarity. Persisting in the project of political resistance and transformation demands comradery both internally and with outside groups (Bos et al., 2005; The Free Association, 2011; Pulcini, 2013). The importance of solidarity to processes of social change has become magnified in today's radically "delinked" world: late capitalist society systematically undermines human connectivity and alliances, to the detriment of projects of political resistance (Layton, 2006).

Solidarity within the analytic community has long been problematic. Factionalism and emphasis on hierarchy have undermined cohesion. Practitioners have often identified more strongly with their particular sect than with the analytic community broadly, in a competitive and combative fashion. Rather than respecting divergent elements of theory and simultaneously upholding commonalities, differing schools of thought have often engaged in acrimonious attack, to deleterious effect (Kirsner, 2000; Mills, 2012; Stepansky, 2009). Books aimed at a general audience gradually disappeared, in favor of factionalized journals that make "incommensurate claims about what psychoanalysis [is] and how and why it purportedly work[s]" (Stepansky, 2009, p. 63). At best, such journals ignore the perspectives of alternative factions, and at worst, they treat them with scorn.

Historical analysis adds nuance to this story. Marginalization, including active persecution from without, fostered insecurity and defensiveness, which in turn contributed to dogmatic certainty, preoccupation with prestige and hierarchy, and isolation within distinct schools. Anxiety-driven dogmatism hindered the development of a flexible, radical, and inclusive analytic sensibility, and contributed to the divide between analytic institutes and universities, as well as to the lengthy exclusion of lay practitioners from analytic training (Aron and Starr, 2013; Jacoby, 1983).

To be clear, I do not think psychoanalysis should—or could—offer some kind of perfectly unified vision. As a critical, unpredictable endeavor, diversity of perspective should anchor analytic discourse. Varied theoretical perspectives, as well as diverse clinical, academic, and sociopolitical traditions enrich the field. Psychoanalysis engages life's thorniest ethical and existential questions, in both theoretical and applied terms, and celebrates complexity, freedom, and mystery. If there wasn't serious debate about its ontology and therapeutic methods, psychoanalysis would cease to be psychoanalysis. Yet this need not preclude a basic shared platform from which to engage the public and outside academic factions. A charitable heterodoxy can, and I believe should, serve as the basis for a reasonably united contemporary psychoanalytic community. Diversity of perspective, anchored in respectful debate, as well as in shared ethical convictions, can strengthen, rather than negate, a sense of cohesion. Emphasis on common core ideas and commitments can foster connectivity across diverse fronts without precluding nuanced theoretical deliberation.

For example, focus on the primacy of attachment and relationship in human development and health in contemporary psychoanalysis has facilitated conversation with the general public and outside academics, including critical, cultural, feminist, and gender theorists. Such cross-disciplinary theorization has in turn invigorated the field. Clinical psychoanalysis understands something of how differences can be bridged and meaningful, affectively experienced solidarity forged. Analytic practitioners and patients work to develop a solidarity strong enough to withstand the tumult of analytic treatment, while flexible enough to allow for change (Benjamin, 1995; Summers, 2013; Thompson, 2017). Such a sturdy, flexible solidarity within contemporary analytic circles might lubricate the field's subversive potential.

CONCLUSION

Psychoanalytic theory and practice in many ways converge with theories of subversion, particularly in terms of the most intrinsic, essential features of subversive phenomena. Psychoanalysis disrupts status quos along multiple pathways: by deconstructing processes of internalization and reification of hegemonic norms and values, psychoanalysis undermines the modern political and economic project of psychological manipulation, commodified subjectivity, and manufactured desire, cultivating a more discerning subjectivity instead. Further, by liberating unconscious, libidinal, and often destructive forces, psychoanalysis unsettles the heuristics and assumptions upon which any given sociopolitical status quo depends. It moves toward an erotic freedom that defies social strictures. Finally, by illuminating paradox and complexity, psychoanalysis contradicts dogmatic certainty, including wearily-knowing resignation—making room, instead, for possibility.

Psychoanalysis also engages ethics, both as an embodied practice and philosophical inquiry. Psychoanalysis can be conceptualized as a discipline of character, in which patients explore and develop their personal ethos through discipline, honesty, openminded receptivity, and the analytic relationship. Meanwhile, analytic thinkers critically and expansively ponder ethical themes, such as the nature and limits of pleasure and reason, the possibility of self-determination, and the origins of subjectivity. At both clinical and theoretical levels, this sort of ethical engagement is perhaps particularly subversive in an era where thinking, in the analytic sense of the term, appears under siege. As political discourse devolves into reactive sloganeering, while narrow instrumental calculation replaces broad knowledge and curiosity in academia, and repression of freedom increasingly and effectively targets the press, thinking, in embodied, receptive, ethical terms, has become a radical act indeed. Defensive, hyperbolic, digitally-mediated authoritarianism across the political spectrum substitutes for the receptive, relationally-mediated thought that psychoanalysis at best exemplifies.

These intrinsically subversive aspects of psychoanalysis have often failed to translate into subversion of actually existing sociopolitical relations, doubtless for myriad reasons—including, perhaps, divergence from more auxiliary dimensions of subversive phenomena. Although clinical psychoanalysis in many ways typifies optimal marginality, psychoanalysis has become hypermarginalized at a broad sociopolitical level. Certainly, analytic theory shares enough vocabulary with mainstream American culture to engage in generative conversation, while analytic ideas also have a long history of unsettling prevailing Western notions of selfhood, rationality, sexuality, autonomy, and so on. Psychoanalysis can be seen to uphold particular mainstream cultural values (e.g., self-expression) while also resisting numerous sociopolitical trends (e.g., automation). And yet, psychoanalysis in the contemporary United States has become divorced from mainstream psychology and distal to radical politics. Regardless of the degree to which this is the result of internal or external forces, psychoanalysis would need greater sociocultural cache to function in a more optimally marginal, potentially subversive fashion.

A first step in movement from a hyper- to optimally-marginalized position would seem to be an interest in doing so—and indeed, analytic thinkers and practitioners evidence a growing desire to engage in sociopolitical discourse and to change the internal culture of psychoanalysis, confronting dynamics of racism, classism, and so on. The present study suggests that a more optimal marginality might also be served by greater solidarity within the analytic community, as well as by a more clear, vocal ethical vision directly linked to sociopolitical issues. Put differently, lack of solidarity and of ethical vision may help explicate the gap between psychoanalysis's seeming subversiveness and its actual impact. Certainly, psychoanalytic theory contains an ethical vision, and analytic thinkers are increasingly engaging ethical and political themes. Still, articulation and dissemination of a fully social analytic ethos has proved difficult. A robust ethical vision that links character pathology and development to culture and politics in sophisticated bidirectional ways might help catalyze psychoanalysis's subversive potential.

NOTES

1. As previously noted, psychoanalysis has in many times and places been anything but antiauthoritarian. I do not dispute the complicity of analytic theory, practice, and practitioners in the perpetuation of oppressive and rigid social norms. I contend, however, in agreement with Aron and Starr (2013) and Jacoby (1983), that authoritarianism in the field represents a perversion, or at least a misdirection or misunderstanding psychoanalysis's essential premises. In other words, while psychoanalysis has been applied with an authoritarian attitude and toward authoritarian ends, I maintain that this contradicts the fundamental tenets of analytic theory and technique.

2. Again, by "ideal terms" I do not mean an unrealized abstraction, but my interpretation of psychoanalysis is a best possible version.

Chapter Three

The Ethics of Psychoanalysis

Ethics offer a supple basis for internal cohesion, as well as a bridge between psychoanalysis and outside groups, movements, debates, and so on. Situating psychoanalysis as an ethical discipline forces contention with sociopolitical issues, and the ethical assumptions at their roots. In order to function subversively vis-à-vis the ethical precepts of contemporary hegemonic American culture, the ethics of psychoanalysis would need to at once affirm and problematize mainstream ethics. The ethics of psychoanalysis would need to converge sufficiently with the ethics of American culture to engage in dialogue, but diverge strongly enough to disturb existing values.

An account of the ethics of psychoanalysis could never be authoritative. Ethics are embodied and dynamic, and do not truly exist a priori. Ethics respond flexibly to evolving circumstances and situated truths. Still, ethical principles and commitments undergird analytic practice and theory, guiding inquiry, research, and treatment. Particular ideas about health, suffering, sanity, and freedom ground psychoanalysis, unifying diverse theorists and practitioners. In constructing a set of analytic ethical principles to serve the purposes of this project, I have loosely followed Aristotle's derivation of virtues in his *Nichomachean Ethics*. This is a whimsical venture. As a professional discipline, psychoanalysis does not have a character per se, nor possess virtues—at least not in anthropomorphizing terms. Ethical principles guide analytic praxis, however, much as Aristotle (trans. 2002) believed virtues guide lived activity.

ARISTOTLE'S VIRTUES

Aristotle (trans. 2002) begins his seminal treatise by asking simply, if less succinctly, "What is a good human? How might we define a life well lived?"

He rejects pleasure straight-away, at least in hedonic terms, as well as external achievement, and any sort of forced action. Although action matters greatly to Aristotle, he believes that to be truly ethical, activity must proceed from internal motivation. Such inner motivation, furthermore, must be felicitous: we cannot be truly virtuous through tyranny, even if such tyranny is internal. Further, Aristotle considers happiness something evaluated over the course of a lifetime, not a momentary state. There is no formula or guarantee. Still, we can strive to cultivate the conditions for happiness to take hold: here enters virtue. While Aristotle readily concedes that happiness has both internal and external dimensions—for the ancient Greeks these two spheres were inherently interrelated—the internal dimension of happiness becomes the focus of his text. He wants to persuade his readers that the cultivation of virtuosity is central to a life well lived.

Virtue (*arête* in ancient Greek) translates literally as excellence. Virtues are both descriptive and aspirational. Virtuousness for Aristotle (trans. 2002) points toward an ideal state, but is in practice an embodied, contextual, and imperfect project of self-development. Although used to guide behavior, virtues cannot be adopted automatically nor used abstractly to differentiate right from wrong. Virtues cannot be cleaved from character—from the difficult work of becoming the kind of person one most wants to be. Like Nietzsche's (1887/1974) will to power, Aristotelian character development involves working patiently and consistently with our innate disposition toward the qualities we seeks to embody. We cannot force ourselves to change, but can consciously consider admirable traits, and practice accordingly.

The question becomes: Which virtues should one hone? Aristotle begins by explaining that he does not know the answer, then derives a list through an amalgam of common wisdom (though problematic, Aristotle suggests this must hold some truth), analysis of individuals he particularly admires, and his own lived experience. He takes pains to emphasize that his list is not beyond reproach, and that virtues in general are neither static nor absolute. A virtue that serves well in one instance may prove detrimental in another. Individuals must take thorough stock of any given situation, weighing actions against any number of factors, and balancing personal and collective goods. For this reason, deliberation becomes the quintessential Aristotelian virtue.

Lest such deliberation sound overly logical, Aristotle suggests that virtue involves harmonizing rational and irrational aspects of the psyche, honoring the gamut of human wants and needs. Because virtues form an integral aspect of being-in-the-world, which involves pathos, art, spirituality, and so on they must be aesthetic as well as instrumental, emotional as well as rational. This means that temperance or moderation emerges as the second definitive Aristotelian virtue. Because of life's vast complexity, most traits are good in some circumstances, but not in others. Responding to life's eternal variety and multiplicity calls for balance. Individuals should avoid getting carried away with any one thing. Indeed, even temperance cannot be applied dogmatically. Some things (adultery, for example) are bad even in moderation, and some situations warrant extremity (such as strong anger in response to grave injustice).

In keeping with this brief sketch, the core ethical principles of psychoanalysis I offer here are neither absolute nor to be mechanistically applied. Certain principles may emerge as more or less salient depending on circumstances, and may manifest differently in different clinical situations, historical eras, and so on. These principles are both descriptive and aspirational. That is, they point toward the political, insofar as they represent a vision of "eudaimonia," but without dictating specific policies. Because ethics are embodied and dynamic, applied by diverse practitioners and impinged upon by various contingencies, any abstract "vision" such as this is at once a reduction and an ideal. Nonetheless, I believe the following contains a meaningful reflection of the values and virtues that undergird psychoanalysis. Following Aristotle, my selection of principles is grounded in my lived experience—as an analytic patient, practitioner, scholar, and trainee. In continued semblance, I also draw on the ethical principles expressed in texts I admire. I am indebted to many thinkers. I would like to stress, however, that the following interpretation of the ethos of psychoanalysis is essentially my own. Although I believe it possesses theoretical mooring, it is ultimately idiosyncratic, and should be evaluated as such. It is a frankly positive vision, reflecting my passion for psychoanalysis. Specifically, the "virtues" or ethical principles of psychoanalysis I elaborate are as follows: the importance of attending to subjective experience, honesty, growth through suffering, care, mutuality, regard for the unknown and the unknowable, reverence, creativity, freedom, and paradox.

THE IMPORTANCE OF ATTENDING TO SUBJECTIVE EXPERIENCE

Psychoanalysis emphasizes internal experience. Analysts express curiosity about patients' inner worlds in full depth and complexity, exploring history and fantasy, conflicts and contradictions. In contrast to manualized treatment, analytic therapists uphold the uniqueness of every person's story (Summers, 2013). By eschewing symptom-based diagnostic categories in favor of holistic, idiosyncratic understanding, analytic practitioners impart a basic dignity to subjective experience (Harlem, 2015; Ogden, 2005).

Through this attention to subjectivity, the analyst hopes to inspire a similar attitude in the patient. Analytic treatment aims toward increased capacity for self-awareness and reflection, regardless of symptomology (Freud, 1938/

1964; Summers, 2013; Wallwork, 1991). In keeping with contemplative and mindfulness-based traditions, as well as with the Aristotelian virtue of deliberation, analytic theory holds that attuning more fully to internal experience stimulates growth and healing. Concerted, ongoing reflection on values, goals, history, and relationships facilitates the development of a sense of meaning, purpose, and commitment (Aron & Starr, 2013). Increased self-awareness can loosen the grip of past experience and internalized social mores, and lead to a reclamation of aspects of psyche previously repressed, denied, or projected (Freud, 1911/1958b; Thompson, 2004). Perhaps paradoxically, close attention to one's self also enriches interpersonal relationships. Instead of viewing attention to subjectivity as indulgent or solipsistic, analytic theorists maintain that self-awareness is essential to compassionate and intimate relationships with others (Summers, 2013).

Superficial and instrumental interpersonal relationships proliferate in today's radically objectifying culture. Lack of genuine durable relationships lead individuals to relate to others narcissistically—as two-dimensional "objects" rather than three-dimensional subjects. In order to relate to others as full nuanced subjects, individuals must first experience being responded to as subjects themselves (Klein, 1935, 1940). Being related to as an autonomous, intrinsically valuable, and emotionally complex being potentiates the capacity to do the same for another person. Thus, in analytic theory, the therapist's curious, receptive attention to the patient's inner world increases the patient's chances of connecting deeply with others (Summers, 2013; Thompson, 2004).

Increased self-awareness also encourages us to reclaim unpleasant aspects of the self commonly projected onto others. Once acknowledged, bad feelings and unpalatable motives don't need to be located in someone else. By exposing the complex, conflicted nature of the psyche, analytic attention to subjective experience also lessens the need to simplify reality, splitting the world into binaries of good and bad, us and them, and so on. Individuals become more tolerant of flaws and limitations, ambiguity and gradation, and less likely to inflict harm out of disavowed feelings and desires. Thus Freud, like Plato and Aristotle, considered self-examination a first-order ethical principle, foundational to success as a parent, friend, neighbor, and citizen (Wallwork, 1991). The catch, from a Freudian perspective, is that self-knowledge requires considerable effort, as well as the help of another person. It is also never complete. The examined life, per psychoanalysis, is more elusive, collaborative, and painful than Aristotle believed (Wallwork, 1991). Attention to subjective experience forms a necessary but insufficient step toward self-knowledge and character development.

HONESTY

One of Freud's primary insights was that dishonesty contributes to psychopathology: neurosis develops when wishes, desires, traumatic experiences, and the like cannot be accepted or metabolized. The analytic subject is warped through love, shame, betrayal, history, and social norms. Its motives are under perpetual suspicion. It thinks it is thinking when it is really rearranging its prejudices. Analytic treatment thus seeks to facilitate a radical sort of honesty, across multiple registers. Honesty can be seen as psychoanalysis's most basic premise and technique (Thompson, 2004; see also Freud, 1938/1964).

Analytic patients are asked to critically and skeptically examine their lived experience, including values, goals, assumptions, desires, relationships, and self-perceptions. Analysis deconstructs motives, aspirations, and automatic, habitual activity (Summers, 2013). Like a good skeptic, the analyst puts even the seemingly obvious up for question, exposing the complexity of the mundane. As Aron and Starr (2013) explain, "[psychoanalysis] seeks to expose and subvert the various binary oppositions that undergird our dominant ways of thinking" (p. 50). Because much of habitual, automatic thinking and values is culturally derived, moreover, psychoanalytic honesty threatens established social constructs, including internalized demands and prohibitions (Layton, 2015; Zaretsky, 2015).

Analytic honesty also moves beyond the realm of critical thinking altogether, suggesting that much of our self-deception lies beyond self-awareness—and proposing a method to subvert this duplicity. Psychoanalysis disrupts conscious, linear reasoning by asking patients to "free associate"—that is, to say anything and everything that comes to mind, however seemingly tangential or irrelevant. Free association strives, in a sense, to catch us unaware. It unearths a range of feelings, fantasies, and memories inaccessible to conscious, willful command, by actively suppressing of our habitual mode of thinking (Freud, 1900/2006). Fundamentally receptive, free association resembles Keats's negative capability (as cited in Bion, 1970, p. 125) and Heidegger's (1959/2010) releasement. The truth free association reveals resembles that of creative projects, dreams, and waking reverie: the kind that emerges when we suspend, at least for a moment, our continual reflexive judgments.

Analytic honesty also contains an interpersonal dimension. The capacity for self-deception at the heart of analytic theory suggests that radical honesty requires the presence of another person. It is a wounded cogito that emerges from psychoanalysis, one forced to confess its rather limited insight into its own motivations. The patient's free association requires another person for interpretation. As the analyst receives the patient's unconscious communications, fleeting dreamlike musings become solvent for subsequent reflection.

The analyst also calls the patient's bluff, bringing to bear their own ethic of honesty (Thompson, 2004). Perhaps the most fundamental goal of analytic treatment is simply to face reality—as contested a term as that may be (Freud, 1911/1958b). The ethic of honesty involves learning to tolerate the "truth" of one's own life—psychic and physical, current and historical—as revealed by the hermeneutic, relationally-mediated investigation that is psychoanalysis (Cushman, 2005). It involves recognizing the false promise of satisfactions which ignore the interpersonal, the real (Wallwork, 1991).

Privacy, secured through a commitment to confidentiality, constitutes an important subprinciple to the analytic ethic of honesty. Invitations to free, candid self-expression can only be accepted if the lurking fear of consequence can be assuaged. Privacy safeguards patients' inchoate reflections in analytic therapy, and permits experimentation with new ideas and ways of being without demanding commitment.

GROWTH THROUGH SUFFERING

Psychoanalytic honesty proves challenging. It involves plumbing the depths of all that is typically too frightening or overwhelming to bear—facing up to the painful circumstances of our lives. Analysts ascribe to a tragic worldview. They theorize a choice, first proposed by Freud (Breuer & Freud, 1895/1956), between hysteric misery and everyday unhappiness, and their method is painful (Carnochan, 2001; Thompson, 1995). Questioning personal and cultural assumptions destabilizes internal structures and external relationships and provokes anxiety. Examining wounded, needy, shameful, aggressive, and repressed parts of the psyche hurts. Reality is often disappointing. Indeed, it is the distress of radical honesty that leads to neurosis in the first place: symptoms often develop through resistance to truth, loss, and pain (Thompson, 2004; see also Freud, 1917/1957a).

Analytic theory sees symptoms as personally meaningful, pointing toward our histories and fears, as well as toward a cure. Naturally, analysts hope that over time, patients' symptoms will remit, but this is not the central preoccupation of analytic therapy—nor would symptom remission yield a perfectly felicitous human being (Summers, 2013; Thompson, 2004). That is, psychoanalysis proposes an endogenous theory of human suffering: we all have sadistic and destructive urges, and our parents (and our analysts, and our realities) are never as wonderful as we wish them to be. Contra utopian fantasies of an engineered society, part of living together, in the analytic vision, is inflicting and receiving pain. Psychoanalysis involves mourning this reality, accepting limits and fallibility, and relinquishing illusion in order to make the best of what we do have and can become (Drassinower, 2003; Wallwork, 1991).

In the frustrating situation of infancy, Freud (1917/1957a) believed satisfaction is first attempted through fantasy. When this fails, however, as it inevitably does, the gap between reality and desire must be acknowledged—and then acted upon. Frustration thus drives change by supplying the requisite motivation. Frustration initiates new ways of being. It is indispensable to eudaimonia: "our possibilities for satisfaction depend upon our capacity for frustrations . . . [in situations of] instant gratification, neither desire nor the object of desire is sufficiently imagined" (Phillips, 2012, pp. xix–xx). If we move too quickly toward satisfaction, settling for cheap thrills or simply denying frustration, we may fail to grasp the truth of desire, and its means of satisfaction. Analytic treatment thus encourages both patient and practitioner to move *toward* the frustration and suffering of symptoms, analysis, and life. Part of this ethic of moving toward suffering, on the part of the analyst, involves radical receptivity to the suffering of the patient. The ethics of psychoanalysis arguably begin in an empathic, emotionally engaged response to the suffering of the other (Orange, 2010).

CARE

Psychoanalysis can be seen to hold two distinct primary aims: to understand the human condition and to promote greater psychic health (Wallwork, 1991). The analytic ethos of care applies to each. Regarding the latter, analytic theory maintains that human health depends on empathic attuned relationships (Summers, 2013). The psychoanalytic subject is often misconstrued as fundamentally selfish—bent, deep down, on hedonic instinctual gratification. Civilization, in this narrative, is primarily repressive—an evil necessary to procure basic security and cultural advance. This theory leads to an inhibitory morality and an appeal to community on the basis of enlightened self-interest. While this picture is not without justification, Freud, opposing Hobbes, believed a society of individuals rationally pursuing private interests would ultimately prove unsatisfying—a recipe for neurosis (Wallwork, 1991). He saw individuals as fundamentally and erotically oriented toward connection with others, and suggested Eros as the proper basis of civilization. Mature love, from a Freudian perspective, involves seeing the other as separate, empathizing with their experience, and working toward their welfare. Such love is essential to human flourishing, individual and collective alike (Wallwork, 1991).

Freud is not a traditional humanist, however, insofar as he rejects ideas of natural goodness (Wallwork, 1991). While he sees Eros as part of our genetic inheritance, its manifestation as mature love requires effort, especially when things have gone awry early on. Intimate relationships may be health-promoting but are also a primary source of psychopathology (Freud, 1917/

1957a). Subjectivity is inscribed in a relational matrix. Past, present, and hoped for relationships, as well as transgenerational transmission of trauma, pervade emotional and psychic life (e.g., Bromberg, 1998; Fraiberg et al., 1975).

People seek therapy because their capacity for love has been compromised, and analytic treatment affords an opportunity to develop that ability (Thompson, 2017). If nothing else, the analyst seeks to provide a receptive, caring other who can withstand the patient's rage, despair, and madness. This is especially true since the so-called "relational turn," which has led to heightened emphasis on transference and countertransference dynamics (Aron & Starr, 2013; Mitchel, 1988). While early analysts sought to maintain neutrality, contemporary practitioners often argue that involvement in the drama of a patient's relational world is inevitable, and facilitates greater understanding of their psychic life (Mitchel, 1988; Ogden, 1992). The analytic relationship both reactivates previous relationships, as internalized by the patient, and affords a new template. In the midst of familiar interpersonal dynamics unfolding in the transference-countertransference matrix, the analyst does not simply repeat previous experiences (Winnicott, 1971). For example, the analyst generally avoids retaliation, substituting "the talionic principle with the principle of grace, returning interpretation for an eye and interpretation for a tooth" (Racker, 1966, p. 66). Over time, ideally, this new experience alters a person's relational expectations and manner of engagement with others. The therapist's care becomes internalized.

In addition to their role in healing, caring relationships also prove central to thinking and learning (Bion, 1962/2004). The capacity to learn from experience and think symbolically hinges on the provision of what Winnicott (1960) describes as "good enough" relationships. As children, analytic theory claims, experience is overwhelming and unformulated, defying comprehension (Stern, 1983). Relationships with caring attuned parents allow this overwhelm to become tolerated and experience to become symbolically represented. A caregiver metabolizes a baby's unformulated experience, and represent it in solvent terms. Being a good enough parent (or analyst) demands close, patient, emotionally engaged listening—an ethic of care (Bion, 1962/2004). Analysts must cultivate caring, intimate relationships with their patients in order to understand them. No amount of knowledge or skill-building, in this view, can supplant the importance of the therapeutic relationship, built together carefully over time (Summers, 2013). Because it takes time to build caring relationships capable of digesting painful feelings and withstanding interpersonal conflict, psychoanalysis a notoriously a long-term treatment.

MUTUALITY

Although imbedded in the ethic of care, the principle of mutuality warrants distinct elaboration. Ideas about intersubjectivity are central to analytic philosophical and epistemic claims. Analytic therapists see familial, societal, and historical dynamics embedded in patients' psyches—and psychopathology (Altman, 1995; Fanon, 1961/2004; Layton, 2010, 2014). This affirms a constructed, dialogic metaphysics: the analyst does not accept and validate the patient's every utterance, but rather uses their own subjective responses to cocreate the therapy session. Psychoanalysis is a direct experience in mutuality (Aron, 1996). Even for patients who struggle to tolerate mutuality, the presence of the analyst inevitably shapes the contours of therapy. A relational context that evokes feelings of desire, dependency, frustration, and need circumscribes analytic dialogues (Freud, 1912/1958a, 1915/1958c). The truth that emerges through analytic therapy is neither objective nor subjective, but rather intersubjective (Stolorow, 1988).[1]

Intersubjectivity as a basic, metaphysical fact is one thing; recognition of interdependence is another. The phenomenological experience of intersubjectivity is a developmental accomplishment. In the presence of sufficiently responsive and loving caregiving, children develop a foundation of interpersonal connectivity and trust. They come to believe in the basic goodness of self and world (Khan, 1979; Winnicott, 1965). The next step involves recognizing the separateness of the mother/Other, who meets the child's needs at times and at times frustrates them. Viewing the other as separate and imperfect allows complex and contradictory feelings toward the same person to be tolerated. It disrupts fantasies of omnipotence, as well as of a perfect love object (Klein, 1935, 1940). This acceptance of fallibility is instrumental to the development of humility, gratitude, and tolerance. Awareness of mutuality encourages more thoughtfulness and sensitivity in interpersonal dealings (Aron, 1996; Summers, 2013; Thompson, 2004).

Again, this is an accomplishment, an ideal. Absent adequate interpersonal experience in childhood, individuals continue to relate to others as extensions of themselves—objects to be controlled, manipulated, and projected onto, to devastating effect (Britton, 1992; Klein, 1940). This kind of relating, which Klein (1935) describes as paranoid-schizoid, resurfaces in moments of stress, even for individuals more accustomed to whole-object relating. We are all prone to omnipotent fantasies, to pretending we don't depend on others, to hating others for frustrating our needs, for disappointing us, for being human.

Analytic treatment, though difficult and uncertain, can provide at least a partial remedy for habitual paranoid-schizoid relating—a pedagogy of mutuality (Aron, 1996). The painful, drawn-out process of analytic therapy seeks change at a characterological level, bringing patients closer to mutuality. A patient can learn to accept their need for their therapist, for example, as well as the therapist's imperfect ability to meet them. A patient can grow to acknowledge the therapist as a separate person with separate needs, while simultaneously holding onto their own experience (Britton, 1992).

That is not to say that Freudian philosophy upholds some sort of kumbaya notion of relationships. Freud (1930/1961) in many ways blamed society for individual psychopathology, positing an animalistic psyche locked in a fundamental antagonism with collectivity. He did not, however, want to dispense with civilization, nor proffer a sixties-era vision of hedonistic self-expression or glorified id. He rather advocated changes in the construction of society (Wallwork, 1991; Zaretsky, 2015). Freud harbored a deep suspicion of the morality of prohibition—of positive behavior motivated by fear of retribution, guilt, and duty. He doubted that the ethical development he advocated could be grounded solely in Kantian reason. As Wallwork (1991) explains, "Freud is in the Aristotelian-Humean philosophical tradition in assuming that in order to guide action, practical reason must be motivated by some desire, want, or interest" (p. 234). His practice alerted him to the dangers of "practical reason isolated from affect, as it is in obsessional neuroses" (p. 235). In other words, Freud sought to ground morality in Eros, as well as in reason, and in Eros of a particular sort, which might be described as a drive toward mutuality.

Most simply, Eros is the life force that exists in dialectical tension with Thanatos, or the death drive—one pole in the eternal drama of construction and destruction, excitation and rest, fertility and disintegration (Freud, 1920/1955). Eros is often construed as a selfish force, or libidinal desire bent on its own gratification. This is partly accurate: Eros is fierce, it is personal, and in many ways opposed to civilization. Psychoanalysis portrays disparate individuals with desires and needs that often compete, and threaten established social orders. Yet this dissenual reality nonetheless drives us toward mutuality. Eros compels active, sensual, sexual participation in the human community (Marcuse, 1955; Wallwork, 1991). For Freud as for Aristotle, human flourishing involves satisfying participation in collectivity.

How Eros expresses itself depends on psychic development. At its best, Eros generates mature love and recognition of interdependence. It fuels the difficult task of working together, across differences, toward a best-possible society (Marcuse, 1955). Eros, if all goes well, "opposes war to dialogue, my wish to murder to the possibility of an intersubjectivity rooted in the assumption of otherness" (Drassinower, 2003, p. 27). The ethic of mutuality points toward this vision.

REGARD FOR THE UNKNOWN AND THE UNKNOWABLE

The idea that much of psychic life lies beyond the realm of conscious awareness, with very real consequences, is central to psychoanalysis's revolutionary applications and ethical implications (Lacan 1992/1986; Critchley, 2007; Zaretsky, 2015). Belief in unconscious processes unites diverse analytic thinkers and clinicians and undergirds analytic theories of freedom, vitality, and creativity (Lear, 1998; Thompson, 2004).

Neither a place nor a thing, "the unconscious" represents a universal and unquantifiable dimension of psychic experience beyond conscious awareness and rational decision-making. Freud first theorized the unconscious in his early treatment of hysterics. He noticed that memories of disturbing events could be banished from consciousness. These memories then reasserted themselves in the somatic symptoms of hysteria, which remitted once the memories were consciously reclaimed (Freud, 1896/1962). As Freud's theory expanded, however, so did his ideas about the unconscious, which grew to include not only actual memories but wishes, fantasies, impulses, and the like, which did not necessarily have to have been conscious at any point. Freud (1915/1957b) noticed that anything contradicting a person's ego ideal was more likely to become or remain unconscious, including intolerable ideas and whole emotional registers, such as anger.

Because what individuals find desirable and despicable is significantly influenced by family and culture, the unconscious carries a weighty social dimension; indeed, one could speak of a social, cultural, or ethnic unconscious (Herron, 1995). Both individually and socially, the restrictiveness and severity of prevailing norms and ideals impacts the nature and extent of repression. Attention to sociocultural dimensions of unconscious process distinguishes psychoanalysis as a form of mental health care, and forms an important aspect of the nexus between analytic theory and radical politics; it marks the analytic project of character development as subversive (Zaretsky, 2015).

Unconscious material often re-presents itself in symptoms. Unpalatable or unthinkable aspects of experience, repressed into unconscious recesses, manifest in adverse consequences. Hence, making the unconscious conscious is central to analytic therapy. The analyst listens to the unspoken, disavowed, avoided, and unknown. Analytic treatment endeavors to help patients make sense of previously unsymbolized experience and tolerate previously intolerable thoughts and feelings. A successful analysis increases a patient's capacity to bear their aggressive and destructive impulses, sexual fantasies, and so on.

And yet the analytic project of increased self-awareness is doomed to at least partial failure (Bollas, 1999). No amount of insight or therapy changes the mystery that permeates personal and collective psychic life. Dimensions of experience always remain outside conscious awareness. Thus, analytic therapy calls for radical honesty but affirms the limits of knowledge, proposing that both making the unconscious conscious and releasement toward the mystery of the unconscious can foster greater psychic health (Bollas, 1999; Lear, 1998; Ogden & Ogden, 2012).

Whichever aspect of this paradox one emphasizes, attention to unconscious processes serves as a foundational, orienting ethic of psychoanalysis: "psychoanalytic experience begins with recognition of the *demand* of the unconscious, the impingement of the *Faktum* of unconscious desire in the form of the symptom" (Critchley, 2007, 66). Perhaps psychoanalysis's most basic ethical goal is to put the subject in relation to its unconscious desire (Lacan, 1986/1992). Psychoanalysis orients toward the mysterious, whether to interpret and understand it or simply to wonder about it. Both patient and practitioner bind themselves to something beyond prediction and control, treating the unknown with receptive curiosity. Pauses, synchronicities, and slips of tongue, generally ignored or chalked up to mere coincidence, are treated as meaningful. From an analytic perspective, "everyone is poetic; everyone dreams in metaphor and generates symbolic meaning in the process of living" (Lear, 1998, p. 31). Regard for the unknown and unknowable reveals this poetry.

CREATIVITY

Attention to unconscious processes both involves and stimulates creativity. Psychoanalysis could never be manualized—nor even approached formulaically. Analytic theory refuses to reduce the psyche to the activity of the brain and rejects the idea that scientific data or technical interventions could ever fully solve the problems of human life. Instead, analytic therapy emphasizes creativity, offering a protected space for experimentation, and responding flexibly to the evolution of each hour. It is in part an exercise in spontaneous play (Parsons, 1999; Winnicott, 1971).

Receptivity is key. Quiet listening allows unconscious communications to be heard. Suspending automatic thoughts allows free association to unfold. In keeping with Heidegger (2002), analytic theory proposes that by relaxing and releasing conscious pathways of thought, new ideas and ways of being are remembered, discovered, or revealed. From the murky borders of conscious experience, new forms emerge. When we can relax, tolerate not knowing, and play with diverse ideas, as yet unthought solutions often develop. Sleep is required in order to dream (Ogden, 2004). The structure or frame of analytic therapy serves to vouchsafe this creative, challenging process of examining and developing oneself and one's life.

FREEDOM

Freud distinguished psychoanalysis from hypnosis and other suggestive strategies through regard for patients' autonomy. Analytic theory emphasizes our capacity to change in desired ways (Fong, 2012; Wallwork, 1991). Although classical theory has been significantly modified by contemporary thinkers, analytic neutrality still aims to free patients' expression from normative assumptions and censure and to make room for as yet unknown possibilities (Bollas, 1999; Lear, 1998; Thompson, 1995).

The freedom psychoanalysis offers is always circumscribed: the psyche is constituted through family, culture, and society, influenced by unconscious processes, and inherently prone to self-deception. Analytic freedom should not be conflated with simple self-expression, willpower, or control. In many ways, psychoanalysis demonstrates how enslaved we can become by addiction, neurosis, restrictive social norms, and the punitive recitations of the superego. Freud's theories undermined Victorian-era notions of self-control used to blame individuals for their symptoms, and his theory of psychic determinism has been used to bolster fatalistic philosophies. Nonetheless, analytic theory upholds a radical freedom. Psychic determinism implies that all mental activity is meaningful, but not that it is directly caused—nor, especially, immutable (Wallwork, 1991). In keeping with hermeneutic philosophy, Freudian determinism locates the psyche in a rich biological, sociopolitical, familial, and historical matrix, but denies the nihilism that can accompany such a situated view. Psychoanalysis suggests that its thickly constituted subject can gain a greater sense of freedom both through attunement to the mystery of the unconscious and through developing itself as a character.

Opening toward or aligning with mystery and possibility, represented by the idea of the unconscious, is crucial to a psychoanalytic understanding of freedom (Lear, 1998; Summers, 2013). Free association seeks freedom *from* assumptions, habit, certainty, and attempts at control, and *toward* the uncertain and as yet unknown possibilities. As Thompson (2004) writes, "The words uttered in psychoanalysis *are determined by one's freedom*, if one understands freedom as that which cannot be dictated" (p. 30). Free association involves letting go of our conscious, controlling egos, in the service of a radical freedom; it "serves the instinctual needs of the self to be created anew, each day, in a freedom of mental life that is unavailable for the organizational aims of a self or a society" (Bollas, 1999, p. 74).

This understanding of freedom has much in common with Christian, Buddhist, and Skeptic conceptions, which propose that freedom arises from surrender or acceptance (Thompson, 2017). Importantly, surrender in these philosophies does not entail a passive or defeated resignation, but rather an open, spacious receptivity, akin to Heidegger's (2002) *Gelas-*

senheit (releasement) and the cosmic resonance Aristotle (trans. 2002) considered essential to human flourishing. It connects to the world beyond the self.

On the other hand, psychoanalytic freedom is quite personal. It involves living with greater authenticity, coming alive to our direct experience, articulating our unique idiom, and the truth of our desire (Lacan, 1986/1992; Lear, 1998; Summers, 2013). This in turn entails becoming aware of material that has been personally repressed, denied, or falsely adopted. Free association may liberate us to a more creative, passionate lived experience, but it must first free us from repression and social programming (Aron & Starr, 2013). Freedom from psychopathology, inherited assumptions, and socially manufactured cravings can be cast a precondition to freer access to authentic desire and a deeper dimension of freedom. Analytic freedom thus entails critical examination of conditions of oppression, including their internal manifestations (Wallwork, 1991; Zaretsky, 2015).

Such a freedom is hard won, at best imperfectly achieved. We can never extricate ourselves from context and contingencies, nor from our inherently limited perspective. Even if freedom is ontologically given, it takes effort to experience. It demands a discipline of character, of which psychoanalysis is a particular version. For all the analytic emphasis on free association, "at certain critical moments, the analysand has to decide he *wants* to look" (Mitchell, 1988, p. 264). The analysand must choose to examine themselves critically. Psychoanalytic freedom does not come through forceful control, but it does entail working on one's self—though working is perhaps too strong a word. Psychoanalysis involves patient, receptive self-engagement, acknowledging limits, losses, and uncertainty, while questioning perceptions and desires. It involves honing commitments and habits, in keeping with one's particular and evolving ethical truths. This process births a certain kind of freedom. Psychoanalysis suggests that "persons can become the sources or causes of their own action, even though they are themselves the products of a complex network of various types of causes extended over time and now hierarchically organized" (Wallwork, 1991, p. 97).

If all goes well, analysis changes us in fundamental ways. It impacts not only symptoms and other surface phenomenon, but also deeper strata—its influence extends to desire, sexuality, values, and perception. It may make a mockery of attempts at conscious or rational determination of fate, but by proposing to influence psychic depths, it introduces freedom even into traditionally deterministic terrain. It suggests that we can alter even irrational and unconscious aspects of our psyches. Thus, in a certain sense, psychoanalysis expands the limits of free will. As Wallwork (1991) explains, although psychoanalysis can be interpreted as "shrinking the realm of moral responsibility by bringing to light new excusing circumstances" (p. 91), it can more accurately be interpreted as expanding moral responsibility by asking individuals to assume responsibility "for those inner inclinations and defenses of which we are not yet conscious" (p. 91)—both prospectively and in retrospect.

PARADOX

Analytic truths are nuanced, paradoxical, multiplicitous, and discordant: love comingles with hate, desire with aversion, and so on. Absolute certainty becomes suspicious, if not impossible. As Bollas (1999) writes,

> To Freud's lasting credit, he never organized his many views of mental life and human relations into a single system of thought. He knew, and he conveyed the fact, that his subject was simply too overdetermined for such systematic organization. (p. 99)

While resolution of psychic conflict is often both desirable and possible, analytic theory maintains that psychic life is essentially dialectical. When a particular aspect of experience is denied, the effort only strengthens the negated quality (Freud, 1920/1955). Thus, celebration of paradox forms an important analytic ethical principle, and one affirmed by many by spiritual and philosophical traditions, including the principle of yin and yang in Chinese philosophy (Cartwright, 2012) and the Dionysian and Apollonian dimensions in ancient Greek philosophy (Nietzsche, 1872/1999).

The ethic of paradox leads toleration of complexity and contradiction to become a goal of analytic therapy. Analysts since Klein (1940) have observed the human tendency to oversimplify experience, to negative effect, and have sought to increase patients' capacity for ambiguity. Through the analyst's curiosity and elaborative receptivity, and the patient's radical honesty, the analytic couple discovers new dimensions within even the most seemingly mundane material. More flexible thinking and greater comfort with different perspectives is one marker of successful analysis (Aron & Starr, 2013; Phillips, 2012).

Not only does analytic treatment foster more dialectical thinking, it also rests on paradoxical tensions. Analytic treatment asks patients to free associate in a boundless, timeless manner, within the firm boundaries of the analytic frame. It encourages patients to dream, fantasize, and believe things possible, and also to face "reality." It both encourages and discourages transference neurosis (Thompson, 2004). It endeavors to make the unconscious conscious—to name the unnameable, think the unthinkable—while also embracing the limits of thinking and the power of mystery (Gentile, 2015). Meaning is both made and deconstructed (Aron & Starr, 2013).

Celebration of paradox does not negate the importance of pursuing truth rigorously nor the possibility of factual knowledge—although psychoanalytic thinking can and does fall victim to the extreme relativity for which postmodernism has been indicted (Cushman, 2005; Mills, 2012). Instead, the principle of paradox emerges from extensive and rigorous thought: from a deliberate bracketing of assumptions and exploration alternative points of view. This ethical precept involves commitment to diversity as such, and belief in the value of dialogue between opposing ideas (Aron & Starr, 2013; Lear, 1998; Wallwork, 1991).

The analytic ethic of paradox converges with Aristotle's ethic of the mean. For Aristotle, equanimity shares with deliberation a special place among the virtues: virtuous activity as such tends to involve a course of action somewhere between excess and deficiency—a course of balance (Aristotle, trans. 2002). Ethics involve considering the infinite variability of circumstances and factors in any given decision, on their own merit and as part of an aesthetic and functional whole. Ethical conduct threads a needle between various extremes and recognizes that every situation is different (Aristotle, trans. 2002). Similarly, the ethic of paradox embraces a dialectical spirit of inquiry, affirms the value of opposing perspectives, and brackets particular truth claims.

NOTE

1. The term "intersubjectivity" is diversely conceived in analytic literature. Teicholz (2001) traces three primary orientations: intersubjectivity as the ontological fact of mutual influence (theorized prominently by Stolorow, Beebe, and Lachmann) intersubjectivity as the developmental accomplishment of mutual recognition (as understood by Stern and Benjamin), and intersubjectivity as emergent, creative shared meaning on the basis of symbolic functioning (which can be understood as an extension of the second meaning, and which has been centrally elaborated by Ogden). My use of intersubjectivity is most consistent with the second view.

Chapter Four

The Ethics of American Culture

In order to assess the interface between the ethics of psychoanalysis and the ethics of contemporary American culture, this chapter offers an interpretation of American ethical mores. Any attempt to explicate dominant American ethical values is limited by the difficulty defining any sort of "mainstream" within the sweeping diversity of the United States, as well as by the intangibility of ethics. Ethical convictions and commitments often remain unarticulated despite their influence on daily life and political decision-making. They evolve in response to changing historical and material circumstances, strategic manipulation, and so on.

As when constructing psychoanalytic ethical principles, I approach the task of delineating mainstream American ethical values with Aristotle's derivation of virtues in mind, drawing on common assertions, relevant literature, and my own experience, as well as systematic value poles. Two texts in particular feature prominently in the following analysis. *Habits of the Heart: Individualism and Commitment in American Life*, presents extensive sociological data gathered by its authors—Bellah, Madsen, Sullivan, Swidler, and Tipton (2008)—as well as historical analysis, integration of comparative literature, and exploration of cultural heroes, myths, and legends. Influential economist Jeffrey Sachs's *The Price of Civilization: Reawakening American Virtue and Prosperity* (2011) includes primary research in the form of informal interviews and hundreds of opinion surveys on American values, in addition to compilations of previously published value studies. The principles I discuss are as follows: successfulness, happiness, productivity, individualism, toughness, rationality, honesty, diversity, freedom, and equality.

On one hand, defining core American ethical values seems especially challenging and problematic in the present moment. In our fractured, divisive political climate, different groups express radically different ethical visions.

Traditional values seem threatened, and reactionary currents proliferate. "Americanness" is being renegotiated to an uncertain end. Thus, defining what America believes in feels like a daunting and ambiguous task.

On the other hand, the increased synonymity between the ethics of free market capitalism and the ethics of American culture over the past fifty years simplifies the project. Although many different value systems operate to significant effect in American cultural life, the ethos of capitalism has largely dominated collective ethical and political life in the United States for many decades (Layton, 2010; Piety, 2004; Sennett, 1998). All ethics and ideologies exist in a material and historical framework that reinforces, weakens, or otherwise modifies them. Ethical visions develop within structural realities. Media and messaging controlled by a powerful elite mold subjective beliefs, desires, and values. Late-stage corporate capitalism has significantly shaped prevailing ideology in this country (Harvey, 2005).

Thus, the following analysis of core American ethical principles emphasizes the ethics of contemporary capitalism, and does so in critical terms. This particular ethical philosophy can be described as "neoliberal"—vague and contested a term as this may be. Neoliberalism describes a distinct, more recent strain of liberalism, sharing the latter's focus on the rights and choices of individuals, centrally including private property, and commitment to democracy and free market capitalism, including a particular interpretation of freedom. Classic liberalism advocated laissez-faire economics and a minimal or "night watchman" state; following the Great Depression, a stronger state seemed important, giving rise to the New Deal and modern welfare state. Neoliberalism in turn developed in response to these trends, advancing policies of privatization, austerity, deregulation and free trade, and also, in contrast to liberalism, a strong state. The neoliberal market state intervenes to protect the integrity of money and private property, and the creation and functioning of markets. As an ethical philosophy, neoliberalism rests on the idea that eudaimonia is best served by "liberating individual entrepreneurial freedoms and skills within an institutional framework characterized by strong private property rights, free markets, and free trade" (Harvey, 2005, p. 2). The ethics of neoliberalism is certainly rejected by many groups, and diversely interpreted, but nonetheless pervade collective life. Neoliberal capitalism has shaped material conditions to such a degree that individual ethical development in some sense cannot help but be influenced.

I also draw on traditional American values and existing cultural reality in the following text. Neoliberalism shares many traditional American values, such as freedom and competition, and has altered these values over time—a process I hope to explicate. I also comment on contemporary cultural trends, including expressions of racism, xenophobia, and so on. I do not, however, focus on right wing extremism. Another caveat: I am describing values, not reality, in this text. For example, equal opportunity can be considered an influential ethical ideal in this county, however far from reality.

SUCCESSFULNESS

Immigrants have traveled to the United States from across the globe in pursuit of the "American Dream": the idea that here, anyone can succeed. The United States has held mythic status as "the land of opportunity," where success is available for the taking (Bellah et al., 2008; Sachs, 2011). Creating the conditions wherein anyone willing to work hard can prosper has exerted a defining influence on collective identity and ethos, and is considered a central function of government (Saad, 2013). In addition to the opportunity to succeed, Americans highly value success itself. Such success generally connotates externally demonstrable accolades and achievements and, especially, financial gain. The opportunity offered in the land thereof is generally conceived as that for material advancement (Bayles, 2015; Piety, 2004).

An American obsession with making money and "getting ahead" has been noted from de Tocqueville (1835/2003) to modern times, and has been exacerbated by neoliberalism (Rubens, 2009). Economic prosperity is a central goal of liberals and conservatives alike. Other goods are certainly valued, but nothing supersedes economic prowess, which functions as an end of itself rather than a means to other objectives, such health care or public works. For example, in a 2009 Pew study, 85 percent of respondents endorsed strengthening the economy as the nation's top priority (The Pew Center for People and the Press, 2009, p. 84), over workers' rights and environmental protections, both of which were supported as independent goods. In a society dominated by capitalism, economic growth can seemingly function as a crucifix to which all competing goods are nailed. Greater employment rates, lower taxes, and economic progress win unfailing popularity, while economic impracticality can spell death for any program, no matter how worthwhile.

Societal devotion to material success is mirrored in individual aspirations and recognition. Americans tend to celebrate the wealthy as paragons of success, rather than viewing them oppressors of the masses, as is the case in many countries. Children are rewarded for impressive external accomplishments from preschool onward (White, 2017). Conversations about wealth have been shifting in the twenty-first century, with disparity increasingly criticized and redistributive and reparative policies gaining popularity. Still, Trump's wealth helped persuade voters of his qualifications for presidency, while liberals fetishize Silicon Valley nouveau riche.

Underlying the ethic of material successfulness lies a longstanding conflation of financial success and happiness (empirically disproven after a baseline threshold). An increase in GDP is associated with a better, happier society, while individuals believe greater material success will make them happier (Sachs, 2011). A second conflation is also at play: using Protestant logic, Americans have long associated material success with being a good person, discussing achievement in explicitly moral terms (Kantor & Streitfeld, 2015; Weber, 1904/2001). In a contemporary example, employees at Amazon traced their persistence under punishing, punitive conditions to morality and self-esteem. Succeeding in a highly competitive, exclusive environment led individuals to feel better about themselves—to experience themselves as disciplined, intelligent, industrious, and worthy (Kantor & Streitfeld, 2015). In a cultural ethos of successfulness, such an internal experience was likely reinforced by other people.

This abiding mishmash of prosperity, morality, and happiness proved fertile soil for neoliberalism's obsessive reductive focus on economic growth (Piety, 2004; Sennett, 1998). The welfare of the polity has been subsumed by the welfare of the economy (Chomsky, 1999). Monetization proliferates in every sphere: "sensuous human existence and morality [are subordinated] to the 'facts' of the marketplace and technical rationality" (Bellah et al., 2008, p. 108). Individuals have become largely defined by their jobs, generating cynical terms such as "homoeconomicus." A spirit of competition, winning, and losing corrupts even seemingly collaborative, nourishing activities: cooking, for example, becomes Iron Chef.

On an individual level, the pervasive adoption of a neoliberal ethos means that the "virtues" of the "free market"—such as competitiveness, flexibility, selfishness, risk-taking, and rationality—increasingly guide ethical thinking and choices (Sennett, 1998). Such traits are valued largely due to their association with success. Being successful has become linked with being hard-nosed and selfish in order to outcompete others in a cutthroat world. It has also become associated with flexibility, as fiscal success increasing demands willingness to adapt to an unstable, unpredictable economy. The inconveniences of changing jobs, reskilling, moving, and cobbling together various tenuous part-time positions are reframed as evidence of the virtue of flexible adaptation. While material circumstances (e.g., the dissolution of social services and weakening of familial and community bonds) reinforce these values, they in turn propitiate economic reality. Externally demonstrable successfulness remains primary to the ethical vision of American society.

HAPPINESS

The pursuit of happiness is inscribed in the Declaration of Independence. It is a fundamental American goal and virtue. The project of achieving happiness forms a constant theme of conversation and the backbone of a thriving self-help industry, not to mention consumer culture more broadly. Above all else,

Americans want happiness for themselves, their children, and their friends. A gross national happiness report now appears alongside the GDP. Indeed, happiness in the United States today may have displaced wealth as the ultimate trophy (Whippman, 2016).

While the American conception of happiness has much to do with prosperity, it also involves more internal and ineffable features. Happiness is often discussed as a private, subjective affair: each individual is responsible for finding happiness and is the ultimate judge of that mission. This can breed anxiety, with some loudly proclaiming their state of bliss and others worrying incessantly, "Am I happy? Am I happy *enough*?" (Whippman, 2016).

Of course, few would dispute the worthiness of doing one's best to enjoy life. Happiness may not be life's most important aim, and it may be better pursued indirectly, but happiness in various forms—joy, peace, eudaimonia—is central to myriad wisdom traditions and ethical philosophies. It is often considered the hallmark of a life well lived. The peculiar aspects of American happiness are twofold, and contradictory. First, happiness is seen as a virtue or personal, subjective accomplishment, rather than as a temporary state, or result of material circumstances, right livelihood, or meaningful activity (Bellah et al., 2008; Gregoire, 2014). Second, paradoxically, happiness is sought compulsively in various experiences and products (Whippman, 2016).

Because happiness for Americans is considered not only a goal but a virtue, happy people are praised and admired, and the unhappy disparaged. Maintaining a positive, cheerful attitude is linked, in ethical discourse, to success and goodness (Bellah et al., 2008). This characterological understanding of happiness can lead to the neglect of sociopolitical and economic dimensions of well-being, as well as intensified pressure to be happy, unrealistic expectations about how happy one can and should feel, and a general aversion to all things difficult, depressing, or disturbing (Bellah et al., 2008; Gregoire, 2014). While at its best, the American emphasis on happiness fosters a playful, youthful, in-the-moment cultural climate, it can lead to a pathologizing of discontentment. Fixation on happiness as a cornerstone of moral virtue and human flourishing—now legitimated by positive psychology—can foster a sort of "hedonic treadmill," as well as to the devaluation of painful, infuriating, and sad thoughts, feelings, and experiences (Gregoire, 2014).

Contradictorily, although happiness is generally conceived as an internal virtue or achievement, it is often pursued though an array of services and products. The American ethic of happiness cannot be cleaved from capitalism, which has a vested interest in keeping citizens titillated, but never satisfied. Satisfaction is antithetical to the ethos of capitalism, as it is only by selling citizens new "needs" that capitalism continues to grow (McGowan,

2016; Streeck, 2017). Consumer capitalism thus both sells and sabotages the happiness project. It may be unsurprising, then, that Americans statistically report chronic unhappiness, despite pronounced cultural emphasis (Whippman, 2016).

PRODUCTIVITY

Americans work notoriously long hours. The question "How are you?" is often answered "busy"—with masochistic pride (Bellah et al., 2008; Piety, 2004; Tolentino, 2017). Productivity is linked to a particular American entrepreneurial attitude, scanning the horizons for creative financial opportunities, and working diligently when opportunity strikes. Courage, initiative, self-reliance, and successfulness are all symbolically associated with productivity. Even psychotherapy is evaluated in terms of efficiency (e.g., Esposito, 2014).

Iconic American heroes are frequently self-made. The narrative of "rags to riches" looms large in our collective psyche—and not without reason. A measure of truth adheres in the idea that, at least historically, for certain subpopulations, sufficient hard work led to considerable prosperity (Bellah et al., 2008). Women, slaves, and native peoples were excluded from this narrative, but in contrast to aristocratic Europe, the young United States offered white men an expanded opportunity to advance themselves through hard work, regardless of birth.

As with happiness and successfulness, productivity is cast as a characterological virtue, vital to self-esteem, and estimation by others. Pride in workaholism is a widespread phenomenon: Americans brag about grueling hours, insufferable conditions, and other sacrifices made for work (Kantor & Streitfeld, 2015; Tolentino, 2017). A connection between industriousness and goodness is ingrained in the American psyche (Gregg, 2016). Hard work is consistently portrayed as crucial to material success, considerable evidence otherwise notwithstanding. In contrast to citizens of other countries, Americans tend to attribute prosperity to personal effort, rather than systemic forces (Bellah et al., 2008; Gao, 2015). Nearly all participants in a 2009 Pew study, for example, affirmed that hard work predicts success in life. This same study cites a pervasive admiration of the rich for working hard. Poverty, on the other hand, is condemned as the product of laziness—a moral vice (Layton, 2014). Those not focused on work are often disparaged as "wasting their life" (Bellah et al., 2008).

This attitude cannot be cleaved from Protestant and neoliberal ideologies. As Weber (1904/2001) notes, a pivotal Protestant innovation was the association of industriousness with godliness; to waste time was the cardinal Protestant sin. Luther proselytized that belief and prayer were insufficient to secure access to heaven. Productivity and material success evidenced membership among God's chosen people. (Hence the quip, "God is coming, look busy.")

Capitalist economies depend upon individual and societal productivity: upon the continual production of commodities and accumulation of capital (wealth), regardless of need or intrinsic value (McGowan, 2016; Piety, 2004; Streeck, 2017). Glorification of work as a virtue vital to success (and anxiety that absent hard work, one will fall into destitution) helps extract the grueling working late hours capitalism demands. Those who succeed under contemporary market pressures increasingly conceive of themselves as professional endurance athletes, pushing themselves to their limits. Advances in technology have exacerbated this trend: modern workplace culture is always on, featuring a proliferation of productivity apps that promise to aid in a constantly improved self-management toward the goal of doing ever more (Gregg, 2016). Individuals are now encouraged to view themselves a unit of continual productivity and monetization: personality commodification and marketing has become pervasive (Maleen, 2018).

INDIVIDUALISM

American individualism is a widely cited and distinctive phenomenon (e.g., Bellah et al, 2008; de Tocqueville, 1835/2003; Gao, 2015; Khzmalyan, 2015). While every society has to negotiate tensions between individual and societal needs, autonomy and attachment, individual rights have consistently trumped collective goods in the United States. Individual aspirations and happiness take priority over social and familial obligations (Bellah et al, 2008; Sachs, 2011). Foreign visitors since de Tocqueville (1835/2003) have remarked on the unique and impassioned quality of American individualism, while a recent Pew Research Center study (Gao, 2015) found that belief in the importance and influence of individuals distinguished Americans from citizens of other countries.

Many Americans consider protecting the right of individuals to behave as they wish the primary purpose of government. Civic participation is considered optional, and social services are often cast as enabling (Sachs, 2011). Meanwhile, individual freedoms are championed across the political aisle, from neoliberal deregulation to back-to-the-land self-reliance to gun control to women's right to choose (Saad, 2013). Countless dollars are spent on quests toward self-realization and personal fulfilment, while childhood is often conceived as a process of progressive individuation. Class, race, history, and indebtedness to social institutions are often ignored in favor of narratives of individual industriousness and innovation. Society is more commonly construed as restrictive or inhibitory than facilitative vis-à-vis individual dreams (Bellah et al., 2008). Even as rhetoric has shifted in recent years in favor of communality, Americans often bulk at objectively positive political policies that are construed as impinging on individual choice (gun control, for example, or the Obama administration's Affordable Care Act). Although since the 2016 presidential campaign, socialist policies have become more popular, for many years, allegations of socialism served to assassinate political candidates and programs (Khzmalyan, 2015).

The American ethic of individualism has evolved over time. Bellah et al. (2008) trace four distinct strains of American individualism: biblical, republican, utilitarian, and expressive. Early Western settlers came to the United States in search of a place where they could worship as they chose, bequeathing a legacy of separation of church and state. These settlers' biblical ethos emphasized tolerance of individual differences and staunch support of individual freedoms. Such support found reinforcement in the republican ethos of the country's revolutionary era. The idea that every individual should have a say in their own governance has endured as an important ethical precept. Of course, in practice American democracy has always excluded large numbers of people. The United States was built on land stolen from native populations and through the labor of women and slaves—none of whom were allowed to participate in democratic society. Exalted American rights have often extended only to white men.

These rights have nonetheless played an important role in American ethical discourse, and came to be defined in increasingly economic terms during the Gilded Age that presaged modern corporate culture. The ethos of "utilitarian individualism" (Bellah et al., 2008) foregrounded a commitment to the ruthless pursuit of individual economic self-interest. As the spirit of free-market capitalism came to dominate American culture, a reductive, materialistic individualism gradually displaced a more robust and emancipatory republican vision (Douthat, 2014). Meanwhile, the "expressive individualism" of the sixties-era cultural revolution championed individuality in artistic or expressive terms. In this paradigm, expressing one's unique self became an important ethical virtue, contributing directly to personal happiness or fulfillment. This strain of individualism has reached unprecedented heights in the age of selfies and social media (Douthat, 2014).

Considered together, these four distinct strands of individualism add nuance to the American ethic of individualism. On one hand, the premise that everyone should be able to express themselves fully and live life as they see fit, provided it does not directly harm others, has attracted immigrants to American soil and idealists to American ethos. The United States has served as a refuge for mavericks and nonconformity. The ethic of individualism opposes the hypnosis of groupthink and the oppression of rigid conventions. It carries tacit regard for diversity: free self-expression implies respect for the gamut of human experience. In political terms, moreover, American individualism points toward deep democracy. Rule by majority is oppressive from the perspective of radical individualism. Rather, each individual voice should be heard and reflected in government. The ethic of individualism can be seen to imply an inclusive participatory community.

On the other hand, American individualism weakens social ties, eroding both the subjective experience of collectivity and actual practices of democratic community (de Tocqueville, 1835/2003). From neighborhood parties and sports leagues to organized politics, civic engagement dwindled steadily over the twenty-first century as utilitarian individualism gained ever greater ground (Putnam, 2000). Robust conversation about the collective good has similarly deteriorated (Sandel, 1982). The results have been disastrous, at least in terms of the cultivation and protection of collective resources and equitable distribution thereof. Layton (2006, 2009) claims that our subjectivity is increasingly pervaded by a sense of what she calls "de-linking," which obfuscates collective responsibilities and resources, fostering both selfishness and anxiety. Utilitarian and expressive strains of individualism have eroded a more progressive and deeply democratic vision. The basic Smithian theory that each individual pursuing their own self-interest has seemingly been proven wrong, but continues to pervade ethical thinking and political decision-making, reinforced by the structure and ideology of neoliberal capitalism.

TOUGHNESS

American individualism has a rugged edge. The ethos of individualism involves being tough, gritty, self-reliant. It entails a can-do spirit that persists at all costs, hardening up in defiance of obstacles. Americans idealize the pioneer, the outlaw, the cowboy, who survive largely through their own pluck—when the going gets tough, the saying goes, the tough get going. The ethic of toughness fosters an individual-versus-the-world mentality, and a spirit of aggressive self-protection: violence lies just beneath the service of this virtue. American heroes often carry a gun, prepared to use it. Politically, the ethic of toughness manifests in glorification of competition and military power, as well as in themes of conquest and combat. Crime is diminished by getting tough, for example, and drug addiction is treated by starting a war.

Perhaps this ethic of toughness emerged in part through the United States' early years of European conquest. Survival in a foreign landscape with no collective regulatory bodies in which to turn demanded self-reliance. Surely individual toughness has become necessary in modern times. Under radical free market capitalism, we cannot count on others to assist us should we fall behind. Nor, in a society of constant dynamism without protection, does a present position of advantage guarantee future success. "Sink or swim" is a common reality for those not insulated by substantial wealth. The absence of a social safety net and resourced communality fuels a sort of Darwinian survival of the fittest 2.0 (Layton, 2016; Piety, 2004; Tolentino, 2017).

If the ethic of toughness has hypertrophied in the contemporary landscape, it has deep philosophical roots. The United States can be conceived as an experiment in a society designed on the basis of the radical Enlightenment-era reconceptualization of human nature. In opposition to earlier Western theories that considered individual life meaningful only in the context of the collective, as well as to religious ideas about the loftiness of the soul, thinkers beginning with Hobbes developed an understanding of the individual as selfish, myopic, and bellicose, more likely to kill others than collaborate. From this perspective, foundational to the United States, society serves to safeguard individuals from each other, in order that they can freely pursue private aims (Bloom, 1987). Such independent pursuits, moreover, in competition with one another, leads to maximal collective flourishing in this theory. Competitiveness becomes a virtue that promotes creativity and innovation. As Piety (2004) writes, Americans constantly "struggle to be fitter than our neighbors and coworkers, whom we have come to view not as a source of companionship and support, but as competition" (p. 107).

Competition as an ethical value became cornerstone to neoliberalism as it gained ascendance over the past half century (Harvey, 2005). Adam Smith's observations about the potential harmony between self-interest and common good, the "law" of supply and demand, and the motivating force of competition became grounds for the dissolution of myriad forms of collectivity and allowing large segments of the population to flounder (Piety, 2004). The modern ethic of toughness justifies rampant disparity: while tragic, poverty indicates a lack of toughness, a lack of virtue. A hypercompetitive landscape inevitably populates with losers (Verhaeghe, 2014). While many of the disaffected protest this vision, successful actors continue to embrace a spirit of "competitive self-improvement, of untiring cultivation of one's marketable human capital, enthusiastic dedication to work, and cheerfully optimistic, playful acceptance of the risks inherent in a world that has outgrown government" (Streeck, 2017, 38). That is, the ethic of toughness and competition persists, extensive criticism notwithstanding.

RATIONALITY

Americans love numbers. To follow the news in the United States is to be practically bombarded by them. We want to ground decisions in data, and believe that once we do, results will follow. The basic idea that if in possession of the right information, everyone would act in rational self-interest, and that this would lead to the best possible society runs deep (Bloom, 1987). It is an essential premise that underlies much of the American estimation of education. Americans consider as much education as possible as a universal good, and, at least historically, invested heavily in public universities and schools. The ethic of rationality also fosters a healthy skepticism, a desire to think things through independently, and a no-nonsense pragmatism that emphasizes action. Another iconic American figure is the calculating business genius, who makes a fortune on account of savviness and ingenuity. This hero's rationality leads directly to their success (Bellah et al., 2008).

The ethic of rationality could be renamed the ethic of science. The United States is in many ways a product, ideologically, of the Enlightenment, and public estimation of reason owes much to the influence of thinkers like Hobbes, Rousseau, and Locke (Bloom, 1987). Faith in reason grounds the ethic of rationality—and, arguably, the entire project of the United States. The ethic of rationality accords with basic scientific premises of objective inquiry, and the application of the findings of such inquiry to real-world situations. Thus, this ethical value would seem to foster thinking.

In recent years, however, the ethic of rationality has often been used to stifle thinking. Thought without supporting data is discredited, often dismissed out of hand, while data is presented as a substitute for thought itself. Americans often appear to believe that issues are as simple as the numbers representing them, or, put differently, that there is no issue that cannot be solved scientifically. Such beliefs may belie a desire to control: to possess enough data to perfectly predict the world around us, and plan accordingly (Cornwell, 2010). The mind, in this view, is a rational prediction machine, in keeping with the philosophy of the Enlightenment. As Bloom (1987) laments, we have "so simplified the soul that it is no longer difficult to explain?" (p. 43). This is of course particularly true in the contemporary digital milieu, which touts data as the pathway to salvation (Kantor & Streitfeld, 2015).

Reliance on data, at the expense of thinking, accords with a long-standing American tradition of anti-intellectualism. The ethic of rationality traces, in part, to an historical privileging of practical wisdom and a mistrust of intellectuals and other elites. Americans claim to trust and admire people we find level-headed, "objective," and action-oriented, while mistrusting people who think too much—or worse, feel too much (Bellah et al., 2008).

Indeed, part of the ethic of rationality involves *devaluing* feelings, as well as aesthetics, spirituality, relationships, and the like, not simply esteeming reason. Strong feelings are cast as a liability, interfering with the capacity to use rational judgment, and therefore to make good decisions (Summers, 2013). Any whiff of the sacred can be similarly spurned, as we increasingly represent, measure, and express ourselves in numbers. Economists have become the gurus of our time (Streek, 2017). The ethic of rationality also faces forward, full of optimism about future progress, and thus fosters a tendency to disregard the past, traditions, the elderly, and the lessons they have to teach (Bloom, 1987).

Ultimately, the ethic of rationality is one dimension of a bigger picture of a country that, on one hand, privileges education, scientific and entrepreneurial innovation, and data-driven, results-oriented strategies. On the other hand, it is part of a country that evidences confused, shallow, absent, and/or hyperbolic thinking about spiritual and ethical matters. The prioritization of rationality and empirical data breeds a false optimism about solving ethical dilemmas through reason alone; the belief that reason can be used to determine value undermines ethical philosophy (Bloom, 1987; Sandel, 1982).

HONESTY

"Honesty is always the best policy," cautions a popular American dictum. As long as you tell the truth, the whole truth, and nothing but the truth, it suggests, everything will be okay. Considered vital to good character and interpersonal relationships, honesty is instilled in school children and demanded in court. Full honesty involves not only accuracy and transparency but also integrity—being rigorous and exacting when developing any particular truth and accepting responsibility for one's knowledge, not hiding behind facile ignorance. Full honesty means being true to truth, fiercely upholding the truths one has come to hold through a process of honest inquiry (Ahearne, 2011).

Historically, honesty has been considered an important collective project in the United States, vital to democratic functioning. Rational knowledge, rooted in honest inquiry, was seen as the proper basis for political decision-making in the United States—as opposed to religion and tradition. Science, in which honesty is paramount, should guide public reason. In the Enlightenment-era philosophy so central to the United States, an educated citizenry creates the best society (Ahearne, 2011; Bloom, 1987). Thus, the ethic of honesty includes a fullness of information: persons in a democracy should have full access to any information available (Bignold, 2012).

Moreover, persons in a democracy should be encouraged to speak their minds candidly. Early thinking about democracy suggested that only by fostering a cultural climate that values honesty, no matter how unpopular, can we combat various forms of tyranny (Mill, 1859/2001). The ethic of honesty entails speaking truth to power. It also involves independent thought. A strong and creative society depends on a cultural climate that welcomes critical, honest thought and speech (Mill, 1859/2001).

The virtue of honesty is under siege in the contemporary world of surveillance capitalism and digital technology, where deception reaps significant reward, rarely with countervailing punishment (Ahearne, 2011; Viner, 2016).

Dishonest portrayal of self and experience has become a glorified pastime, fabricated news a thriving industry, and hidden use of private data an economic staple. The neoliberal ethos of cutthroat pursuit of self-interest has long undermined honesty, removing impediments to dishonesty beyond fear of being caught (Piety, 2004). While honesty continues to be touted as a fundamental moral precept, the ethos of contemporary capitalism in fact condones and rewards dishonesty and corruption.

Trump's rise to power encapsulates this paradox. Nuanced, fact-based political debate has long been displaced by hyperbolic media-driven manipulation of public sentiment, but the brazen dishonesty of the current administration and its assault on the press makes it difficult to maintain democracy as an American ethical principle. Yet despite Trump's obvious dishonesty and corruption, voters in the 2016 presidential election often claimed his honesty as a selling point. His direct, no-nonsense, tell-it-like-it-is self-characterization resonated with many Americans (Cheney, 2016). That is, the ethic of honesty has deep roots and enduring moral pull in the contemporary United States, while also being ravaged by surveillance capitalism and "politainment."

DIVERSITY

Early waves of immigrants traveled to the United States in search of a place they could express minority views, and they have been followed by generations seeking refuge from intolerance. The United States is a nation of immigrants, and contending with difference has long been a collective reality. The idea that everyone, regardless of religion, nationality, and the like should be welcome underwrites the American dream (Bayles, 2015). The image of the United States as a melting pot looms large: in this metaphor, difference creates a rich and colorful cultural tapestry of perspectives, traditions, and so on. A diverse array of people and ideas is considered vitalizing, a catalyst for creativity (Mill, 1859/2001). Differences between people and between groups of people should thus be honored (Bellah et al., 2008).

Indeed, from the earliest years of the US experiment, diversity of opinion has been central to its ethos of democracy, the antidote to the omnipresent threat of tyranny by majority, and protected by the first amendment. According to pioneering understandings, only when the gamut of perspectives is expressed—and frequently and fiercely debated—can democracy truly thrive (Mill, 1859/2001; de Tocqueville, 1835/2003). Diversity of perspective sharpens collective thought. Even if one rejects the belief that diversity fosters dynamism and combats the tyranny of public opinion, however, different beliefs, values, lifestyles, and the like are to be tolerated in this country, absent flagrant harm, as a condition of democratic freedom. Americans express pride in the ability to voice unpopular opinions and "agree to disagree" without loss of mutual respect. Indeed, estimation of divergence runs so deep that it can breed mistrust of homogeneity. The conformist is often denigrated as boring and cowardly, and the maverick celebrated as courageous and exciting. At its extreme, the ethic of free, diverse expression can undermine consensus and condone reprehensible views (Bellah et al., 2008).

The ethic of diversity exists alongside deep-seated racism, xenophobia, and other expressions of bigotry, now on horrific display via the Trump administration's blatant assault on minority and marginalized groups. A deadly intolerance proliferates. The ethic of diversity has always lived in tension with various and violent forms of exclusion, intolerance, and hate, however. The United States was founded through the genocide of Native Americans and the dehumanizing cruelty of slavery. Anti-immigrant rhetoric is as old as immigration itself. White supremacy and misogyny are part of our collective history, if particularly pronounced in the current era.

While bigotry certainly does not require assistance from capitalism, it is no secret that our economic operating system breeds insecurity and divisiveness (Verhaeghe, 2014; Wolff, 2016). Capitalism creates economic hardship and precarity and illusions of scarcity. It requires a class of unemployed, and pits poor and working groups of people against each other. The case can be made that Trump's victory has as much to do with capitalism and class politics as with racism (e.g., Frank, 2017; Williams, 2016). Intolerance is also now abetted by digital platforms that facilitate the contagion and escalation of extremist views (Berger, 2016). Digital technology and its use in surveillance capitalism threatens diversity from a different angle as well: the quest to profit from predicting human behavior actively fosters conformity. In the behavioral futures market, creativity and diversity become the enemy (Rushkoff, 2019). Thus, although celebration of diversity remains important to ethical discourse in the United States—indeed, it has served as a moral anchor for resistance to Trumpism—our contemporary cultural climate makes including diversity as a core American ethical principle problematic at best.

FREEDOM

The tenet that each individual should be free to live as they choose is a linchpin of hegemonic ethics, political discourse, and cultural identity, past and present, left and right (Bellah et al., 2008; Harvey, 2005). Freedom and threats to freedom elicit passionate activity, from guns to abortion, economics to foreign policy. Early European pilgrims' pursuit of religious freedom across dangerous waters has been mythologized, while the inalienable right to liberty prefaces the Declaration of Independence. We admire and celebrate the pilgrims, the revolutionaries, and other heroes for their willingness to fight, even to death, for place where everyone can be free. Certainly, "the land of the free" has always been largely a myth: US history is a tale of enslavement and oppression, while xenophobia, racism, and authoritarianism proliferate in contemporary culture. On the other hand, however, the Unites States has often offered refuge to those fleeing oppressive regimes, and freedom of expression remains relatively high. At least in theory, the American constitution enshrines the freedom to speak, write, worship, and organize however we choose, without fear of repercussion.

Ethical values in general elude precise definition, but the American conception of freedom is particularly evasive, used in diverse ways, to further diverse ends. However, common noteworthy features include the fact that the predominant American version of freedom is a so-called "negative" interpretation. Positive theories of liberty view freedom as something achieved through collaborative participatory social frameworks and processes. Freedom takes effort, and is protected by government. By contrast, negative theories of liberty consider freedom a natural, given state, which government threatens. Models of negative liberty view government regulation, and often collective decision-making more broadly, as inherently inhibitory vis-à-vis freedom (Arendt, 1954). At the heart of negative theories lies an antagonism between the self and the social order, tracing to Enlightenment philosophers such as Locke, who postulated that individuals originally existed in a free "state of nature," but were unable to meet more than very basic needs. They thus entered "social contracts" that allowed for the development of civilization, but diminished freedom along the way (Ferry, 2011; Sachs, 2011). Another way of saying this is that in the United States, freedom it seen largely as an individual phenomenon, threatened by the collective.

In keeping with this view, American discourse on freedom emphasizes self-expression and self-advancement. Freedom involves removing obstacles to personal achievement, pleasure, and choice. The ability to do and act as one chooses is considered both the evidence and condition of freedom. Society, therefore, if acting in the service of freedom, should facilitate freedom of choice, and the best strategy is to remove restrictions. Freedom is conceptualized as "the right of each individual to be left alone by others and by the government" (Sachs, 2011, p. 36). Collectivity and the responsibilities of citizenship (e.g., appropriate taxation based on income, self-initiated education about the social ailments, concern for future generations), by this logic, become an imposition on freedom, a form of enslavement.

Theorization of freedom as the removal of responsibility and constraint serves the interests of corporate capital, and has been actively shaped by proponents thereof (Harvey, 2005). In another example, capitalism's advocates' dexterity in manipulating public sentiment, neoliberalism reinterprets the breakdown of civil society and of functional governmental organizations and regulation as, "the arrival of a free society built on individual autonomy, and . . . as historical progress out of an empire of necessity into an empire of freedom" (Streeck, 2017, 46). Americans today evidence a tendency to treat all regulations and limits with a skepticism that borders on phobia, and regulation of markets or capital is considered particularly offensive. Even in the shadow of an alarming recession linked directly by experts to lack of regulation, Americans assert that government regulation does more harm than good (The Pew Center for People and the Press, 2009, p. 42). This view of freedom has not always prevailed, however.

Historically, the project of designing a society of maximum freedom involved greater complexity. Negative individualistic conceptions of freedom were at a time tempered by an ethos of civic engagement and distributive justice, as well as a willingness to abide by collective decisions. Being a citizen in a democracy was seen as a privilege, and one accompanied by responsibilities. For democracy to work—for political freedom to be sustained—citizens must participate robustly. This involved learning about issues, engaging in public debate, campaigning for elected officials, voting, abiding by the outcomes of this process, and involving oneself in community projects (Bellah et al., 2008; Putnam, 2000). Of course, such participation was always voluntary, and tenuous as such (de Tocqueville, 1835/2003). Still, civic participation was considered vital to freedom: even if freedom was largely conceptualized in individual, Lockean terms, the idea that individual liberty required a high level of political activity ran deep. Further, an ethic of fairness in outcome or distributive justice balanced notions of unfettered individual freedom (Bayles, 2015). Democracy historically involved concern for the welfare of all citizens, motivated in part by the idea that large numbers of insufficiently cared for and uneducated citizens spelled political disaster. Freedom of any given individual in a democracy hinged on the freedom of all.

This is not to deny that the American ethic of freedom has always revolved around ideas of unrestricted personal choice. Rather, personal freedom was seen as contingent upon democratic processes was balanced by competing principles like fairness (Bayles, 2015). Collective processes were considered indispensable to creating the conditions in which individual freedom could flourish (Arendt, 1954). In contrast, today's narrow, radically privatized freedom precludes collective decision-making, and thus a fuller freedom to meaningfully, collaboratively shape the world we inhabit.

EQUALITY

In opposition to traditional European hereditary social classes, the United States was built on belief in the capacity and deservedness of every white male to participate in his own governance. Both the exclusion of women and people of color from this vision, and broad acceptance of the idea of moral equality in today's world may obscure the radical nature of the statement "All men are created equal" in 1776. At the time, the idea that every white man's voice deserved to be heard, and that no door should be closed to such a man on account of birth formed a progressive vision (Gosepath, 2011; Samuelson, 2012).

Although society fails dramatically and irresponsibly to live up to the ideal of equality, Americans consistently express belief in the ethical import of equal opportunity and equal treatment under given circumstances (Mitchell, 2016). Belief in equal treatment applies particularly to the justice system and the workplace—violation of antidiscrimination laws often results in stiff punishment. Contemporary issues and movements that spark moral outrage, such as Black Lives Matter, gay marriage, and transgender rights draw on the principle of equal opportunity and intrinsic worth as central to the moral compass of the United States. The premise that no one should be discriminated against on account of race, gender, age, or other demographic variable evokes passionate response among large groups of people.

Of course, the fact that these issues and movements are issues and movements speaks to simultaneous rejection of the principle of equality by large groups of people, as well as to overtly racist and sexist policies. As with the ethic of diversity, the ethic of equality exists alongside countervailing and intersecting structural forces and subjective attitudes. For all its progressive rhetoric, the US Constitution was designed to serve the interests of land- and slave-holding elite, and has succeeded in its mission. The law has been and continues to be used to actively uphold inequity (e.g., Gilman, 2014; Hertz, 2014; Menand, 2019). Women, poor people, people of color, and other minorities have never received equal treatment, and in the contemporary United States, demographic variables such as gender, race, and class radically impact life outcomes (e.g., Gilman, 2019; Gunn, 2019). Gross economic disparity is a defining feature of this country. And yet, belief in the moral imperative of a "level playing field" or "equal opportunity" is embraced even by conservative Americans—at least for US citizens (e.g., Ariely, 2012).

The purported ethic of moral equivalence and equal opportunity, if this can indeed be claimed as a core contemporary American value, represents a narrowing of the principle of equality over time. Historically, the principle of equality, in theory if not in practice, invoked fuller notions of justice and fairness, including universal education and a modest standard of living. Correcting structural inequalities and providing basic services was considered important to a just and fair society, and resulted in programs aimed at distributive and substantive justice (Gosepath, 2011). Today, however, although certain compensatory and public service programs endure, gross inequality and injustice are broadly tolerated as the fair outcome of what is cast as a free, meritocratic society. Contemporary egalitarianism centers around opportunity and procedural justice, to the exclusion of substantive equality. Absent gross violation of equal treatment, vast inequity appears morally defensible in this interpretation of equality (Bellah et al., 2008; Stiglitz, 2013). All evidence to the contrary, many US citizens seem to believe that all Americans receive equal access to the market and equal treatment in the courtroom, and that these provisions are adequate to the ethic of fairness (Bellah et al., 2008). Behind this view lies the neoliberal belief that individual successes and failures, rather than structural inequalities, fundamentally produce disparity.

Neoliberal rhetoric counterposes equality and freedom (Hayek, 1960; Nozick, 1974). In the neoliberal view, any program or policy that disrupts the free market becomes suspect; the individualism and particular conception of freedom that offered neoliberalism such fertile soil in the United States has also been used to inhibit discourse on equality and justice in substantive, collective terms. Individualism impedes our perception of history and context, racism, and classism, and therefore the moral imperative of combating structural inequality (Layton, 2006). When we view success and failure as the result of individual effort rather than sociopolitical forces, there is little incentive for distributive programs. A sacrosanct, negative ethic of freedom furthers this trend, retarding willingness to make sacrifices on the basis of the common good. If everyone has the right to live however they choose, and no one is allowed to tell anyone else what to do, it is difficult to legislate projects that entail sacrifice in the service of others, and to develop a broad, shared picture of the common good (Sachs, 2011; Sandel, 1982).

Despite the relatively impoverished scope of the principle of equality for many decades, issues of distributive justice and economic equality have recently gained greater traction. The 2008 financial crisis and responses such as Occupy Wall Street helped draw attention and outrage to inequity. Donald Trump's rise to power has reinforced this trend, both through his overt favoring of the 1 percent, and through the bigotry he has inflamed and exposed. Prejudice and its material impact have been receiving more attention in media and public discourse. Manifold difficulties involved both theoretically and pragmatically in legislating economic fairness endure, but distributive justice as a part of the American ethos of equality appears to have at least regained footing in popular discourse (e.g., Horgan, 2019). Meanwhile, the vast and historically consistent inequity in the United States, centrally including racism, means that equality as a core American ethical precept can only be understood in abstract and circumscribed terms. The principle of equality, despite its important role in US history and ethical discourse, has been understood and applied in an unconscionably limited sense. As with diversity, equality warrants inclusion in a discussion of American ethos, but cannot be fully claimed as a moral value under existing circumstances.

Chapter Five

Psychoanalytic Ethics in Contemporary Culture

The disruptive dialogue at the heart of subversive processes means that the subversive lies relative to the mainstream. Subverting existing sociopolitical relations entails an optimally marginal interface with existing norms and values. To function subversively in the contemporary United States, then, psychoanalysis's ethical vision would need to both affirm and negate hegemonic ethos.

As embodied, pervasive, and often unconscious, ethics prove hard to define. Ethics unfold in the mundane—in our bodies, in our daily lives—yet are linked to broader values and vision, and processes of domination and rebellion, stasis and change (Foucault, 1975; Heidegger, 1927/1962). The ethical visions presented in this text cannot capture the complexity, totality, and materiality of ethics. They do not convey the phenomenological experience of ethics, and thus risk reducing ethics to ideology. Nor do they reflect the heterogeneity of both American society and psychoanalysis. These visions are rather simplified abstractions, filtered through my own particular perspective. Still, I will compare these two ethics in an effort to understand psychoanalysis as a potentially subversive phenomenon in contemporary American culture. At least from a cursory view, what stands out most about the two paradigms at hand is their difference, with which I will begin. I then move to points of relative confluence: psychoanalysis is both a product of and influence on Western culture, and substantial similarities exist between these two visions. Finally, I discuss constructs that are shared, but distinctly conceived in each paradigm, thus affording a particular opportunity for optimally marginal ethical engagement.

POINTS OF DIVERGENCE

Subjective/Internal—Objective/External

Clinical psychoanalysis concentrates on subjective experience, asking patients to introspect at length and in detail. Analytic theory claims reflecting on ourselves—our feelings, our work, our relationships, our values, our histories, our minds—as conducive to human flourishing. Absent critical reflection, we are prone to neurosis: we repress aspects of ourselves, or inadvertently repeat the past. Not only does analytic theory uphold the value of introspection for the individual, it also suggests that attending to subjective experience is important to cultivating tolerant, compassionate, fulfilling relationships with others (Summers, 2013; Wallwork, 1991).

In contrast, the ethos of American culture emphasizes material achievement. Externally demonstrable success, including the accumulation of wealth, is fundamental to the American Dream. The Declaration of Independence's provision of the pursuit of happiness appears widely interpreted as the pursuit of tangible accomplishments and prosperity. Our heroes are celebrities from sports, entertainment, and finance. Unbridled financial growth is a chief aim of government across the political spectrum (Bellah et al., 2008). This external focus has only intensified in the digital era, which disrupts introspection and externalizes private moments, encouraging a commodification of every aspect of experience. The frantic pace and hyper-competitiveness of contemporary life further undermines attention to subjectivity (Peltz, 2005).

Of course, subjectivity and materiality are both ineluctable dimensions of human experience. Ethical philosophy must attend to each, as well as their interrelation. American culture does not wholly negate the value of introspection, nor does psychoanalysis ignore the importance of external circumstances. Still, the ethos of psychoanalysis opposes that of American culture along these lines. This opposition applies to policies and programs that reduce human relations to transactions, as well as to philosophies such as positivism and proceduralism that denounce the importance of subjective experience. It also extends to mainstream psychology or "behavioral medicine," which emphasizes observable behaviors and symptoms, standardization, and manualized treatment protocols. Perhaps most fundamentally, psychoanalysis contradicts conceptualizing the self as a unit of production, consumption, and marketing. Instead, psychoanalysis upholds a mysterious and related self—a source of pleasure, creativity, and connection.

Productivity—Thinking

Related to emphasis on material success, productivity forms a core American ethic: a life well-lived comes through accomplishments, which demand productive activity (Bellah et al., 2008). This ethic has strong moral overtones: Americans praise those perceived as hardworking and productive, and chastise anything less as indolence. Self-worth has become intimately linked to productivity, a goal in and of itself (Layton, 2016).

If the ethic of productivity arrived with the pilgrims, it has been sedimented through the logic of capitalism, which demands constant high-level productivity to produce the surpluses that sustain class domination. Productivity eclipses quality and other ostensibly more important aims. We privilege short-term over long-term thinking, and action over thinking, period. Thinking about past is particularly maligned: the ethic of productivity concentrates on the future, especially in the ascendant behavioral futures market (Piety, 2004).

Analytic therapy, by contrast, is inefficient, and produce nothing tangible. While certain results may be hoped for, analysts refrain from predictions, much less guarantees. They encourage patients to speak without agenda (Freud, 1912/1958d; Thompson, 2004). That is, in a world of incessant multitasking, psychoanalysis discourages even uni-tasking. This attitude stems from an ethical vision that emphasizes the importance of free thinking and free speech—including adequate time and space for such speech and thoughts to unfold—as well as from analytic regard for the unknown and unknowable. Listening to unconscious communications involves slowing down and becoming quiet; receptivity to the mystery of being entails a sort of openness or lack of structure (Bollas, 1999, 2007).

The analytic privileging of contemplation and open-ended dialogue—of thinking for the sake of thinking—contradicts not only the hegemonic American ethic of productivity, but the ethos of neoliberal capitalism broadly speaking (Layton, 2009, 2016; Summers, 2013). Psychoanalysis counters the frantic pace of contemporary life, questioning our constant doing, and expanding our capacity to perceive, think, and play, rather than our capacity to produce more things. Analytic treatment leads us to wonder why we do the things we do, and whether we want to. In contrast to our forward-facing culture, moreover, clinical psychoanalysis privileges history, considering the imprint of the past in the present, including the structural, transgenerational dimensions of mental health.

The Power and Role of Reason

To the extent that Americans do value thinking, it is thinking of a rational, linear, efficient sort. We valorize factual information and calculative thought, which are threatened by feelings and other nonobjective phenomena. The ethic of rationality blunts aesthetic, spiritual, and emotional concerns, seeking to ground all decisions in data (Bloom, 1987; Summers, 2013).

By contrast, analytic theory paints reason and its putatively objective data as circumscribed and problematic, maintaining that things are often more complex than they seem, and exposing the tendency of biases, prejudice, moral values, and the like to masquerade as reason (Wallwork, 1991). The psychoanalytic conception of the unconscious indicates that we will never know everything. Even in the hypothetical context of a more perfect reason, psychoanalysis maintains the importance of affect, intuition, and negative space in navigating reality (Bollas, 1999; Lear, 1998). Psychoanalysis thus repudiates prevailing aspirations toward a data-driven reality, questioning the idea of objective knowledge as such, and whether rational decision-making, to the extent that this is possible, would produce the best possible society. The ethics of psychoanalysis firmly oppose techno-utopian thought.

Immediate Gratification—Growth through Suffering

Happiness is a ubiquitous and primary ethical consideration. The nature and relative importance of happiness are different matters, however. In the prevailing American view, happiness is a first-order evaluative concern in relationships and employment, a right inscribed in the Declaration of Independence, to be pursued at whatever cost. In addition to a goal, happiness is also a virtue: the ideal American self is perpetually positive. Such an understanding of happiness has fostered a culture of immediate gratification and hatred of limits, as well as a clinical psychology that pathologizes even minor distress. We want to be happy at all times (Gregoire, 2014; Whippman, 2016).

In analytic theory, happiness all the time is neither possible nor desirable. Both the suffering caused by external circumstances and the suffering we cause ourselves is considered inevitable: one thing we can count on is pain (Carnochan, 2001; Wallwork, 1991). Such suffering motivates change. Without frustration, creativity and maturity stagnate. We fail to learn what suffering has to teach, to our own detriment (Phillips, 2012). Analytic practitioners thus move *toward* suffering: symptoms are seen largely as markers of overwhelming psychic pain, which analysis helps us tolerate.

Limits, in analytic theory, on happiness among other things, are both unavoidable and instructive. Analytic therapy helps patients accept limits, relinquishing illusion in the service of a richer reality (Drassinower, 2003). Thus, from an analytic perspective, the prevailing American ethos of happiness is a recipe for disappointment and contains dangerous illusions of omnipotence. Whatever happiness, immediate gratification, and the evasion of pain and negative feelings affords comes only at significant cost.

POINTS OF CONVERGENCE

Diversity

In analytic theory, repressing or dissociating aspects of our psyche or lived experience leads to psychopathology. Psychic health involves diversity. Analytic therapy thus helps patients accept the gamut of thoughts, feelings, and desires, however inconvenient, and tolerate the ambiguity and contradiction that often accompany such complexity (Aron & Starr, 2013; Thompson, 2004). Similarly, American cultural ethos casts diversity as grist for creativity, possibility, and growth. Everyone is encouraged to find and articulate their unique voice—indeed, nonconformity is considered something of a virtue (Bellah et al., 2008). Both traditions value diverse expression, and both tend to emphasize difference rather than sameness. Heterogeneity is seen as the child of freedom and the parent of creativity (Thompson, 1995).

In spite of this, however, both psychoanalysis and American society evidence conformist, dogmatic, and oppressive tendencies. American culture has long been plagued by a "tyranny of the majority" (de Tocqueville, 1835/2003), while analytic training institutes often foster a rigid and cultish thinking (Kirsner, 2000). Both American and analytic communities evidence superiority and self-righteousness, readily maligning anything "Other." Different individuals, groups, and opinions are often pathologized. What is analytic and what is American are too often narrowly defined and rigidly policed, precisely to the detriment of the diversity both ethical visions uphold. Analytic treatment and theory for many decades concentrated nearly exclusively on affluent, white, heterosexual, cisgender patients, and whiteness continues to exert a defining influence on both analytic and American cultures.

Ambivalence about diversity is thus something analytic communities share with mainstream culture. Such ambivalence helps explain the reality that the principle of diversity contradicts many of the basic facts of American society and analytic communities. This includes blatant discrimination and disregard for difference, but also more subtle phenomena. For example, in the contemporary United States, the idea that people behave in essentially predictable ways has become hegemonic, and is essential to the panoply of data-driven approaches to marketing, politics, and so on, as well as to formulaic approaches to mental health care. Acceptance of surveillance, even the threat of which stifles free expression and fosters conformity, as indispensable to contemporary capitalism has similarly become dominant. Because predicting human behavior has become capitalism's latest frontier, conformity is increasingly, forcefully sought by powerful companies (Rushkoff, 2019; Zuboff, 2019). At best, however, the ethic of diversity contained, if also contradicted, in both analytic and American ethos, resists the bigotry and xenophobia of the current era, as well as the myriad inhibitory and homogenizing pressures of modern life. Instead, it advocates an embracing tolerance and full, unconstricted expression.

Equality

The principle of equality, however ill-aligned with reality, forms as a notable dimension of the United States' ethical vision. This principle has varied over the course of history, at times broadening to include broader notions of distributive justice, but today centers on ideas of fair treatment and basic dignity. For example, contemporary ethical discourse suggests that everyone should be treated equally before the law, and that each person should be able to pursue whatever life they desire. This ethical precept rests on the idea of intrinsic and universal moral worth—a notion also upheld by psychoanalysis. Through the principles of care and of attention to subjective experience, analytic theory affirms the inalienable value and dignity of every person. Meaning inheres in each person's story, and each deserves careful attention. Moral worth persists regardless of psychopathology (Harlem, 2015).

This spirit of equality and dignity opposes the dehumanizing forces of globalized capitalism, as well as the instrumentalism and technocentrism that pervades pseudo-progressive social thought. In the ethos of late-stage capitalism, lives are expendable, interchangeable: the layoff of a thousand people here is compensated for by the creation of a thousand new jobs, elsewhere, in the future. Similarly, visions of an automated future contradict the ethical precept of equality as intrinsic worth by denying individuals autonomy, and the dignity autonomy affords. As in the aristocratic model rejected by founders of the United States, an engineered society revokes the right to self-governance. The principle of equality thus counterposes the ethics of neoliberalism and contemporary surveillance capitalism.

That the ethics of the latter have flourished in the United States points to the fact that the ideal of equality has always existed alongside gross inequity and exclusion, reinforced, in turn, by capitalist economics. Ideas about the virtue of competitiveness and self-sufficiency undermine efforts at reparation and distributive justice, while racism and xenophobia violate basic dignity. Psychoanalysis, for its part, operating within the logic of capitalism, has too often been a treatment solely for the privileged, perpetuating inequity just like American society.

Honesty

Honesty features prominently in moral discourse in the United States. Deeply rooted in Christian teachings, honesty is considered vital to interpersonal relationships as well as one's relationship with one's self. Honesty is seen to form the basis of effective communication, upstanding character, the project of authenticity, and even democracy itself. The ethos of democracy includes the idea that free, honest discourse is integral to collective flourishing. Democratic society thrives through honest exchange—including accurate information. The "informed citizenry" essential to democracy depends on honest communication.

Honesty is arguably *the* ethic of psychoanalysis (Thompson, 2004). No matter how painful or seemingly irrelevant, analytic therapists ask for free expression. Dishonesty breeds neurosis, and honesty, health. Just as legislators strive to protect free speech in American society, analytic practitioners protect free speech in the consulting room, through privacy, neutrality, and trust. Psychoanalytic honesty also contains a collective dimension. Interpersonal relationships potentiate a fuller honesty than can be achieved alone.

In an era of fake news and glorified corruption, upholding honesty as an American ethical value is problematic at best. A long-standing cutthroat entrepreneurial ethos that accepts whatever means necessary to succeed has reached new heights in Silicon Valley's "fail forward" mantra (Taplin, 2017). Thus, although included as a point of convergence, honesty also serves as a point of divergence between the ethics of psychoanalysis and of American culture—or, perhaps, as a point of optimal marginality.

POINTS OF OPTIMAL MARGINALITY

Individualism

The United States was founded as a haven for individual freedom—the repressive capabilities of government and stultifying potential of collectivity lies deep in national consciousness. American individualism portrays independence as a virtue, dependence as a vice, and involves prioritizing personal aspirations and happiness over collective flourishing. Individuals are expected to assume responsibility for themselves and their lives, and are neither obligated nor entitled with regards to others (Bellah et al., 2008; de Toqueville, 1835/2003).

Psychoanalysis also champions individual expression and autonomy, but in different terms. The ethic of attending to subjective experience involves recognizing the uniqueness of every person, and facilitating greater authenticity and autonomy (Summers, 2013; Thompson, 2004). Even in the contemporary climate of two- and three-person psychologies, analytic therapy typically involves focusing on individual patients in a private space. Practitioners' primary ethical obligation lies with individual patients, and treatment outcomes are evaluated along individual lines. Congruently, analytic publications tend to focus more on individuals than on groups, and extending psychoanalytic ideas to culture and society has often proved problematic

(Volkan, 2014). At least historically, analytic theory often posited a fundamental antagonism between individual and societal needs. Although mindful of both, on the balance, analytic theory has tended to advocate for the former, suggesting, at the least, that a healthy society cannot be built on the coffin of individual freedoms (Aron & Starr, 2013; Wallwork, 1991).

Thus, in many ways, the ethos of individualism in psychoanalysis converges with that of mainstream American culture. Analysts' belief in the importance of attending to subjective experience and encouragement of authentic self-expression validate hegemonic ideas about individual worth and self-actualization—indeed, psychoanalysis helped swing the Western cultural pendulum in this direction in the first place (Zaretsky, 2015). Both analytic and American ethics hold that healthy societies cannot grow from repression, manipulation, and forced conformity, but rather require dignity and autonomy. Both advocate self-development and freedom of expression as ethical goods. While such development and expression look different in each vision, both agree that working on oneself is critical to human flourishing. This means that both psychoanalysis and mainstream American culture can readily be used to uphold neoliberal notions of rigidly bounded selfhood and imperatives toward self-management. Both can obfuscate links between the personal and the collective, risking blaming individuals for their suffering and enlisting them in a process of self-surveillance and self-discipline, to the detriment of collective action (Cushman, 1995).

On the other hand, analytic theory asserts that subjective experience is largely socioculturally constructed, postulating mental illness as a shared concern, and therefore broadening the scope of responsibility for individual psychopathology. Analytic treatment exposes the presence of the other in the deepest reaches of the self, and highlight the importance of interpersonal relationships to development and health (Aron & Starr, 2013). In an analytic view, we are dependent and interdependent beings, and recognition of this fact is a sign of maturity: we have a mutual ethical responsibility toward one another, and embracing this responsibility is a move toward health (Wallwork, 1991; Zaretsky, 2015).

Analytic theory thus presents a paradoxical understanding of individualism, affirming subjective experience and individual agency, but also locating interpersonal relatedness and responsibility at the heart of development. Psychoanalysis problematizes individuality as such and proposes a cure through care and connection. It upholds the value of both individuality and relationships, autonomy and interdependency, conceptualizing mental health as both a personal journey and sociocultural product. Analytic theory warns against the dangers of conformity, as well as those of isolation and fantasies of omnipotence. Analytic practice encourages accepting responsibility for ourselves, but also recognizes our interdependence.

By offering this circumscribed, dialectical ethic of individuality, psychoanalysis relates in an optimally marginal way to the hegemonic American principle of individualism. Analytic theory and practice validate the importance of individual subjective experience, dignity, and autonomy, in keeping with cultural estimation of individuality, while also observing the contextual, interdependent nature of subjectivity, and challenging us to balance individualism with greater focus on relationships and collective processes. If individual experience is radically socially conditioned, then we cannot fully attend to subjectivity without attending to politics and culture; civic participation becomes essential to individual flourishing. This particular combination of affirmation and problematization offers a meaningful opportunity for dialogic change.

Freedom

Freedom is central to the national identity, politics, and ethical vision of the United States. Freedom to say and do whatever one thinks and desires forms the foundation of the American dream. Free self-determination is seen as a birthright, present in a fantasied state of nature, and impinged upon by the constraints of society. Lifting restrictions, regulations, obligations, and so on thus enlarges freedom. Conversely, collectivity, particularly in the form of government, threatens freedom. And yet freedom in the United States is also wedded to democracy: the best reconciliation between the ethical imperative of individual freedom and the necessity of living together, in this vision, lies in universal participation in governance. Freedom entails political agency, and can be undermined by its lack. Although political participation today has become essentially individual and voluntary (e.g., voting), civic engagement remains a tangible dimension of the American ethic of freedom.

Psychoanalysis also contains an ethic of freedom. Analytic theory suggests that individuals can change in ways both unpredictable and desired, largely through the particular discipline of character clinical practice affords. While we will always be embedded in culture, a successful analysis allows a patient to gain a greater sense of freedom with regards to imposed ideology and social norms and to forge alternative ideas.

At the same time, analytic theory suggests that freedom involves relinquishing conscious control and surrendering to something beyond our ego. Greater freedom emerges through aligning ourselves with the mystery and possibility of indeterminant and unconscious substrates of experience. Free association frees us both from self-censure and conscious control, and to the creative (and often destructive) possibilities of the unconscious. Psychoanalytic freedom requires both discipline and surrender, critical thinking and appreciation of mystery. Freedom demands both developing ourselves as characters and honing receptive, noncontrolling engagement with the world.

Freedom also emerges in the context of limits. The psychoanalytic subject is thickly constituted, and its freedom circumscribed. As Mitchell (1988) states: we "[create] a work of art through our lives, but with a limited pallet" (p. 255). Free association and character development occur in the context of innumerable impingements.

Although psychoanalysis and mainstream American society share an ethical commitment to freedom, analytic thinking about freedom differs significantly from the hegemonic paradigm. To begin with, analytic approaches to freedom entail effort, well beyond the removal of social restrictions. Analytic freedom involves examining the many ways we participate in our own enslavement—the ways we avoid liberty, and enjoy subjugation. It involves assuming responsibility for our freedom. By contrast, to the extent that hegemonic ideas about freedom do involve effort, such effort entails freeing ourselves from other people: fighting against the constraints of collectivity and the demands of interpersonal relationships. Primarily, however, freedom in hegemonic discourse is innate, absent political repression. It is also relatively absolute.

Although certain concessions must be made in the service of collectivity, free individuals, in the American ideal, can lead whatever life they choose. Freedom is doing whatever one consciously thinks one wants. Freedom is thus tinged with omnipotence, fostering a phobic reaction to limits and dependency. In psychoanalysis, the human subject is inevitably bound by history, biology, and society, and dependent on the natural world and other people for survival. Analytic freedom in large part derives from a suspension of conscious control; the ego occupies quite different places in these two hermeneutics of freedom.

Yet in many ways the ethical principle of freedom in psychoanalysis corroborates the hegemonic American interpretation. Most abstractly, both psychoanalytic theory and American cultural mores posit freedom as vital to human flourishing. Freedom is an intrinsic good in both visions, and also instrumental. Free association and free speech, respectively, produce a generative analysis and engaged, dynamic society. Moreover, both psychoanalysis and dominant culture focus on freedom in primarily individual terms. In a certain sense, both analytic theory and American cultural wisdom also position freedom as an ontological given, existing in a state of nature, or unconscious dimensions of the psyche. Society alienates us from this innate freedom, which we gain greater access to when we mitigate social interference.

In another sense, however, both psychoanalytic and American theories of freedom contain a collective dimension. Freedom in the United States manifests through democracy. Democratic processes safeguard freedom. While the concept of democracy has been impoverished in modern times, at best, it entails vigorous, challenging, ongoing dialogue and compromise in the service of a collective freedom. Analytic therapy, meanwhile, implicates us in each other's suffering, and therefore in each other's freedom. Analysis is a process by which we recognize that the characterological and ethical grounds from which the question of freedom becomes possible is interpersonal. The particular attitudes, character, values, commitments, desires, and manner of perceiving reality we gradually develop is indivisible from our experience of freedom, and also from our relational world.

This rich thinking about the collective vicissitudes of freedom is often neglected by both analytic theory and mainstream culture. Like the hegemonic American assertion that political participation is indispensable to the maintenance of freedom, psychoanalysis's elucidation of the interdependent nature of freedom readily recedes from the foreground. Analytic theory risks reifying a conception of freedom in which "a liberation is promised, but [this] is an entirely isolated, apolitical, individual liberation, which at bottom, of course, is no liberation at all" (Cushman, 1995, p. 68). On the other hand, analytic theory offers a nuanced understanding of freedom that might help advance cultural and political discourse on the relationship between individual and collective liberation. Psychoanalytic theory and practice both support and contradict the hegemonic American ethic of freedom, rendering solvent ground for generative, optimally marginal dialogue.

CONCLUSION

As an ethical philosophy, at least in terms of the abstract principles presented here, psychoanalysis appears well suited to engage the prevailing ethos of American culture in a potentially subversive, optimally disruptive fashion. Actually doing so would require psychoanalysis to occupy a position of optimal marginality within contemporary culture. Because ethics are embodied and pervasive, subversive contact with any given dominant paradigm demands substantial reach. Psychoanalysis would need to become more salient in contemporary culture to function subversively vis-à-vis reigning ethical mores. Analytic theory and practice would need to become broadly viewed as a valuable lens in social, political, and economic dialogues. The current hyper-marginalization of psychoanalysis is a complex and historical phenomenon; greater relevance might be served, however, by firmly situating psychoanalysis as an ethical discipline, in the Platonic tradition, and by actively engaging sociopolitical issues from this platform. Reclaiming a truly social psychoanalysis that listens to and learns from diverse and marginalized voices and offers a complex understanding of the interrelatedness between psyche and society might provide greater traction. As discussed, analytic thinkers appear increasingly willing to engage the world outside the consulting room, including ethics. If psychoanalysis's edge, so to speak, lies in a critical analytic social psychology firmly rooted in its particular ethical vision, this edge has become more conspicuous within analytic circles in recent decades. Greater valence would afford this edge more traction.

Chapter Six

Concluding Reflections

This project began with curiosity about psychoanalysis's radical elements, as well as conformist and oppressive tendencies within the field. It hypothesized that psychoanalysis could be both counted and discounted as a subversive phenomenon, and has indeed elaborated myriad subversive dimensions of analytic theory and practice, while also pointing to barriers to these qualities translating into broader impact. Psychoanalysis is a circumscribed, fallible tradition focused on the individual subject. The ethical precepts imbedded in analytic theory and practice are cultural and historical artifacts whose "moral and political meanings are contingent on how they function in a particular society" (Cushman, 2015, p. 427). Such meanings have often functioned to perpetuate oppressive norms and values. I would not want to exaggerate psychoanalysis's radicalism.

Indeed, despite rich resonance between psychoanalysis and subversive phenomena, psychoanalysis's subversive potential often remains just that. In the contemporary United States, clinical analytic training and practice exist on the fringes of mainstream mental health care; psychoanalysis is commonly considered a relic—an antiquated antecedent to behavioral medicine. Meanwhile, academic psychoanalysis is largely confined to enclaves within other fields. Psychoanalysis's perceived sociopolitical relevance is generally limited to its own adherents. Numerous, synergistic, and historical factors explain this situation (see, for example, Aron & Starr, 2013; Jacoby, 1983; Stepansky, 2009; Zaretsky, 2015). The present study highlights the role of elitism, dogmatism, and factionalism, as well as insularity and reluctance to participate in broad social and ethical discourse.

As a discipline that challenges habitual thinking in favor of radical complexity and open mindedness, it is unsurprising that internal discord has plagued analytic communities. Psychoanalysis is both a theory and a practice, with diverse epistemic and ontological roots. This is in many ways generative—a measure of heterodoxy would seem indispensable to psychoanalysis as such. Yet such heterodoxy need not preclude a robust, coherence basis for solidarity, nor lead to the bitter infighting that has marked the history of psychoanalysis. Recent efforts to build a culture of theoretical pluralism express a desire for greater cohesion, but factionalism and theoretical contradiction persist with analytic circles (Garfinkle & Steinkoler, 2015; Stepansky, 2009). Vague constructs like "the relationship" often thinly mask underlying epistemic and ontological disagreement (Mills, 2012). The legacy of analytic institutes' tendency toward elitism, moreover, focusing on internal hierarchies and treating primarily affluent patients, also continues to inhibit psychoanalysis's subversive functioning (Kirsner, 2000).

The suffering of marginalized and minority groups remained largely outside the analytic purview for many decades; analysts concentrated on individual patients and intrapsychic processes with little regard for context and material circumstances. Analytic therapists and theorists often turned away from political engagement (Botticelli, 2004; Cushman, 1995; Jacoby, 1983; Kirsner, 2000). The project of analytic social psychology faltered, with a distinctive analytic vision of human flourishing, suffering freedom, and so on, occluded from public imagination. Although analytic thinkers now increasingly engage the outside world, this often entails a reductive subjectification of structural, political, and economic problems, rather than a nuanced analytic social psychology that meaningfully links the intrapsychic and interpersonal to the sociopolitical and ethical. Contemporary psychoanalysis has transitioned from a "one person" to a "two person" psychology, but has yet to fully incorporate culture and society, or to reflect the diversity of contemporary society (Walls, 2004). Even the recent turn to ethics in analytic circles remains largely focused on the clinical dyad.

Nonetheless, analytic theory and practice converge with the essence of subversive social change on multiple counts. In the contemporary United States, ethics, in the Platonic-Aristotelian tradition, seem central to subversion. First, in the context of sophisticated psychological manipulation, engineered conformity, personality commodification, and seductive digital distraction, cultivating a collective ethical subjectivity capable of self-observation and critical reflection—of resisting the status quo—seems crucial to progressive politics. Second, considering the monopolizing dominance of neoliberal ethos, a compelling alternative ethical vision also seems fundamental to radical change.

Contemporary society thwarts agentic, rebellious subjectivity. It frustrates deconstructive, antinomian, and complexity dimensions of analytic freedom. A breakdown in thinking marks contemporary politics across the political aisle. Neoliberal capitalism tightly regulates not only work, but also leisure or free time, foreclosing critical analysis and reflective spaces through its long productive hours and hypnotic entertainment. Both industry and the industry of culture suppress thinking (Horkheimer & Adorno, 1944/2002). This is true now more than ever with the ascendant industry of digital technology and behavioral futures actively endeavoring to automate behavior and eclipse thought—tech companies' profit increases the more thoughtless and predictable they can render human conduct (Rushkoff, 2019; Zuboff, 2019). Digital capitalism also demands a sort of personality commodification and marketing antithetical to analytic character development. In a world where material resources are largely controlled by a powerful elite, we are forced to mine our selves for a living—we have become the product in our modern economy. At ever younger ages, we mold our subjectivity through the algorithm of cultural capital and profitability (Maleen, 2018).

Through its dissolution of protective institutions and connectivity of all kinds, moreover, contemporary capitalist culture promotes a sense of pressure and precarity short-circuits spacious ethical reflection. Individuals constantly and anxiously self-monitor, fear of failure looming, always looming. Foucault's panopticon has become a reality, the culmination of the modern project of control through surveillance. We are always being watched. Such conditions work against the difficult, radically honest reflexivity of subversive ethical engagement. Surveillance breeds defensive perfectionism. The ego engages in a desperate, anxiety-ridden struggle to be flawless, anathema to the messy, vulnerable self-exploration of autonomous ethical development. In order to freely experiment, we must feel at least partly insulated from consequence. Another way of saying this is that privacy allows us to develop as ethical subjects: being able to make the wrong choices allows us to make the right ones (Phillips, 2012). Surveillance, identity marketing, economic precarity, manic activity, and incessant entertainment all inhibit subversive politics.

Widespread disintegration of intimate, private relationships further undermines subversive ethical engagement in the present moment. The logic of global capitalism, especially in its latest digital form, is one of exchangeability, displacement, and atomization. It weakens social bonds and collaborative projects of all kinds—including political resistance. Although this may seem paradoxical in light of the putative connectivity of the digital era, enriching human relationships is precisely not the point of new technologies. Digital capitalists profit by drawing our attention away from our immediate surroundings and relationships, and by automating an ever growing number of human interactions. Business growth plans often focus on eliminating employees. Screens relations increasingly replace human ones (Rushkoff, 2019; Zuboff, 2019). This threatens subversive processes, which rely on relationships, from the interpersonal connections pivotal to individuals changing their minds to the solidarity of political organizing and successful social movements.

The urgency that marks the present—including climate change and the humanitarian crises in its wake—intensifies resistance to collective agentic ethical discourse. In an overwhelming and chaotic world, ceding power to authoritarian leadership or to a vision of an engineered society becomes compelling. Projects of technological salvation proliferate on the left as surely as political strongmen and manufactured consent on the right. In light of the right's success in manipulating public sentiment, moreover, counter, leftist ideological manipulation becomes compelling.[1] Given the gravity and severity of current political and environmental crises, it is tempting to tighten social control through restrictive legislation, increased surveillance, and technological sophistication,[2] and to act, period, as if more manic doing were an ipso facto solution.[3] Across the political spectrum nuanced, collaborative, creative thinking has been increasingly replaced by blindly repeated sound bites and rigid, reactive morality. Dogmatic self-righteous moralism, once the purview of the political Right, now permeates the political Left as well (Baily, 2018; Dolan, 2018). Left- and right-wing authoritarian and techno-solutionist tendencies in contemporary society threaten the autonomy vital to subversive processes. Both are essentially strategies of control that deny the importance of agentic and relational ethical development. Both miss the crucial import of thinking, in an analytic sense of the term and impede our capacity to solve the difficult problems of our time.

By contrast, psychoanalysis, as a method of inquiry and an embodied practice, promotes a critical, liberatory subjectivity capable of observing and at least partially transcending its conditioning. Psychoanalysis deconstructs dominant customs, rhetoric, and values, and disturbs their automatic internalization. It disturbs the assumed ethos that upholds the status quo. It elaborates a vastly complex and paradoxical subjectivity that resists any single, narrow, static perspective. It connects to never-fully-tamable mysterious, unconscious, and libidinal processes.

Analytic treatment fosters honest, spacious, and creative reflection on ethical themes, offering an unstructured, unmonitored space, free from the pressure to know and to act. The sanctity of therapeutic confidentiality allows analytic treatment to exist outside the contemporary panopticon, permitting a radical honesty and experimentation. It makes room for the previously excluded, marginalized, unknown. The freedom of privacy—freedom from judgment, from record, from ramifications—allows thoughts and feelings to develop in full and flexible ways. It permits wild, potentially transgressive discourse. Psychoanalysis involves a commitment to human dignity, and the autonomy that commitment demands. This marks it as an open-ended, organic processes, with unpredictable and often disturbing results—it can be called a dangerous method. Indeed, the freedom psychoanalysis offers does not necessarily make society safer, more equitable, or more efficient. Instead, psychoanalysis offers an unruly but deeply human freedom that rejects all versions of an engineered, automated society, all forms of a social straightjacket.

In keeping with the tradition of virtue ethics, the analytic discipline of character development is inescapably difficult, and rooted in interpersonal relationships. It involves confronting our illusions and fears about ourselves, our histories, and so on, which requires the help of another person. It centers on the eternal, infinitely complex question of how to live, which inevitably includes other people. Relatedness and dialogue are the foundation of the psychoanalytic edifice, indispensable to thinking, learning, well-being, and change. Analytic therapy is an exercise in the sort of mutual recognition and genuine conversation threatened by myriad cultural tendencies and essential to subversive politics. Analytic theory understands truth as an historically and collectively negotiated process that hinges upon good enough relationships. Truth is contextual, embodied, and relational. It evolves as we do. Establishing relationships, listening receptively, and thinking together about complex and challenging ethical themes is central to change—personal and political alike.

As demanding and deeply uncomfortable as talking across our differences about the things that matter most to us, this lies at the heart of progressive social change from an analytic perspective. In keeping with the theory of optimal marginality, subverting the sociopolitical status quo requires disruptive contact with difference, with historical and interpersonal trauma, but also empathic connection. Subversive forces deconstruct and agitate, but also integrate and contain. As analytic clinicians recognize, change entails frustration, discomfort, and contact with difference, but also relies on feelings of safety, respect, and connection.

In the sociopolitical arena, subversive optimal marginality involves dissonance and resonance vis-à-vis prevailing ethical discourse. Subversive phenomena disruptively engage hegemonic ethos through a process of simultaneous affirmation and provocation. Surely there are many valuable responses to current social and political catastrophe, including trenchant analysis of material circumstances and economic operating systems, and active involvement in existing political structures. Subversive engagement with prevailing ethics and ideology also seems imperative. Neoliberal capitalism, arguably the defining force of our times, is based not on facts, but on beliefs, systematically promoted by America's wealthy elite in the second half of the twentieth century, in the hopes of restoring concentration of wealth and power to prewar heights. These hopes have exceeded expectations: the contemporary United States is an exceedingly stratified society (Harvey, 2005). What confounds many thinkers is why so many of those suffering most under present circumstances support policies and politicians that exacerbate them. Certainly, partial explanation lies in the reality that seemingly self-defeating choices often make considerable immediate material sense. For example, supporting the interests of a corporation upon which one's livelihood depends is a perfectly rational decision, even if that corporation is exploiting your labor and bankrupting your community (Chibber, 2016). But ideology is also key. Broad swaths of the American population have been persuaded, via costly effort, to adopt particular ethical principles that strongly influence political decision-making. These principles include the sanctity of the free market, the precedence of the economy over all else, and the sovereignty of the individual and of private property (Harvey, 2005). Neoliberal ideology has been successful at least in part because it strategically deploys deeply rooted American ethical precepts such as freedom and individualism. These long-standing ethical values have been coopted by neoliberal rhetoric: they have been narrowed and rigidified, in the service of a particular agenda. Freedom has become reductively conflated with free enterprise and militarism. Individualism has been used to obscure class politics, defund social services, and obscure mutual responsibility.

A primary tenet of hegemonic American ideology and the power it serves is that There Is No Alternative (TINA): whatever the costs of corporate capitalism and liberal democracy, these remain the best possible alternatives. It has been strikingly persuasive. TINA engenders a sense of futility and deadness, and breeds repetitive hopeless material choices. The political Left, for example, bemoans the current paradigm, its critiques are acute and convincing, yet it consistently fails to articulate an animating substitute. A cynical, impotent inevitability inhibits a bold, progressive vision. The Right, meanwhile, also castigates the status quo, but its solution only exacerbates the effects of late capitalism. Effective resistance to the contemporary status quo must transcend its frame of reference, offering compelling and plausible alternatives (Fisher, 2009; Harvey, 2005; Chibber, 2016; Rorty, 1998). Promoting an alternative ethical vision is an urgent task on the political left, yet efforts often amount only to a more humane version of liberal capitalism.

Psychoanalysis offers one possible alternative ethical vision. The ethics of psychoanalysis, as elaborated in this text, have the advantage of relating to hegemonic ethos in an optimally marginal fashion. That is, the ethics of psychoanalysis at once affirm and contradict reigning cultural values. Psychoanalysis shares sufficient conceptual overlap with mainstream culture to facilitate dialogue, but also contains enough distance for forceful critique. Certain ethical principles, such as the intrinsic and instrumental importance of diversity, are shared, while others, such as the relative importance of internal experience and external achievement diverge sharply. Values like freedom and individualism, shared across psychoanalysis and American culture, offer a particular opportunity for disruptive discourse. Although Freudianism disturbed many traditional Western ideas, analytic concepts also shaped our contemporary landscape. Psychoanalysis is rooted in Western philosophy yet in many ways antithetical to contemporary capitalist society.

This means that the ethical vision psychoanalysis contains is well poised to confront prevailing ideology while still championing values like freedom and individualism.

Beyond the particular ethical vision it contains, moreover, psychoanalysis promotes a sense of possibility that loosens the grip of TINA. Psychoanalysis begins with receptive curiosity: nothing is ever merely one thing. There is always more to learn. Attention to mysterious, unconscious, and libidinal processes reveals new horizons. Fidelity to free association, embodied experience, and emergent desire, stimulates creativity and challenges habits and assumptions. Although radically conditioned, the analytic subject, through effort, can change in fundamental ways. Deconstructive, antinomian, and complexity threads of psychoanalysis all promote a sense of freedom, aliveness, and potential might help subvert the entrenched ideology that reifies existing sociopolitical relations.

Again, realizing this potential would require that psychoanalysis become more salient in contemporary society. Psychoanalysis's ethical vision would need sufficient cultural traction to engage in subversive discourse at a broad level. This would entail, at minimum, analytic thinkers and clinicians continuing to challenge narrow-minded, elitist internal dynamics, and to engage the outside world in complex ways, from conferences and training programs to public discourse to cross-disciplinary study to active political struggle. A subversive analytic social psychology would learn from diverse and marginalized communities, listening receptively to and participating robustly in contemporary struggles and conversations, and offering theoretical insights that help make our present moment more intelligible and negotiable.

Ethics, in the Platonic tradition, offer a useful foundation for such engagement. Conceiving psychoanalysis as an ethic in the tradition of Plato and Aristotle links psychoanalysis to social and political concerns without wedding it to any particular political agenda. Like virtue ethics, psychoanalysis does not delineate criteria for determining right and wrong action, but rather investigates, in a dynamic and embodied fashion, the eternal question, "How to live?" Analytic therapists observe a microcosm of political and cultural life—the nexus of the personal and the political, the poignant and painful struggle to live well. Witnessing in intricate detail the subjective and relational damage wrought by structural, material, transgenerational forces creates a unique position from which to link intimate concerns to broader ethical frameworks, deconstructing "normative unconscious processes" (Layton, 2015) and asking questions of hegemonic culture in a critical, potentially subversive fashion. Viewing psychoanalysis as a discipline of character tethers analytic theory to the embodied, radically complex individual subject, and at the same time to a broad vision of human flourishing. Although at present, psychoanalysis is hypermarginalized, with its radical potential often remaining unrealized, I hope this study helps elucidates the nature of psychoanalysis's subversive edge, and how that edge might be sharpened.

NOTES

1. See Lakoff (2004, 2006) for an elaboration of this perspective.
2. See Bellah et al. (2008) for an analysis of the contemporary Left's shift from a strategy of agentic, grassroots social change to one of top-down sociopolitical engineering and control.
3. See Featherstone, Henwood, and Parenti (2002/2018) for an analysis of the pressure to act—and the need to think—on the contemporary left.

References

Ahearne, J. (2011). Honesty. *American Scientist*, 99(2), 120. Doi: 10.1511/2011.89.120.

Akhtar, S. (2018). *Mind, culture, and global unrest: Psychoanalytic reflections*. New York: Routledge.

Althusser, L. (2014). *On the reproduction of capitalism: Ideology and ideological state apparatuses* (G. M. Goshgarian, Trans.). New York: Verso Books. (Original work published in 1970.)

Altman, N. (1995). *The analyst in the inner city: Race, class and culture through a psychoanalytic lens*. New York: Routledge.

Anderson, W., Jenson, D., & Keller, R. (Eds.) (2011). *Unconscious dominions: Psychoanalysis, colonial traumas and global sovereignties*. Durham, NC: Duke University Press.

Antinomian. (n.d.). In *Online etymology dictionary*. Retrieved from: http://www.etymonline.com/index.php?term=antinomian.

Arendt, H. (1954). *Between past and future*. New York: Penguin Books.

———. (1958) *The human condition*. Chicago: University of Chicago Press.

———. (1963). *Eichmann in Jerusalem: A report on the banality of evil*. New York: Viking Press.

Ariely, D. (2012, August 2). Americans want to live in a much more equal country they just don't realize it. *The Atlantic*. Retrieved from:https://www.theatlantic.com/business/archive/2012/08/americans-want-to-live-in-a-much-more-equal-country-they-just-dont-realize-it/260639/.

Aristotle. (2002). *Nicomachean ethics* (J. Sachs, Trans.). Newbury, MA: Focus Publications. (Original work written in the fourth century BCE.)

Aron, L. (1996). *A meeting of the minds: Mutuality in psychoanalysis*. New York: Routledge.

Aron, L., & Starr, K (2013). *A psychotherapy for the people: Toward a progressive psychoanalysis*. New York: Routledge.

Badiou, A. (2001). *Ethics*. New York: Verso.

Bailey, R. (2018, March 8). Tracking down the elusive left-wing authoritarianism. *Reason*. Retrieved from: https://reason.com/2018/03/08/tracking-down-the-elusive-leftwing-autho/.

Bayles, M. (2015, October 10). How the world perceives the new American dream. *The Atlantic*. Retrieved from: https://www.theatlantic.com/international/archive/2015/10/american-dream-world-diplomacy/410080/.

Bellah, R. N., Madsen, R., Sullivan, R. M., Swidler, A., & Tipton, S. M. (2008). *Habits of the heart: Individualism and commitment in American life*. Berkeley: University of California Press.

Benjamin, J. (1988). *The bonds of love: Psychoanalysis, feminism, and the problem of domination*. New York: Random House.

———. (1995). *Like subjects, love objects: Essays on Recognition and Sexual Difference*. New Haven, CT: Yale University Press.
———. (2004). Beyond doer and don to. *Psychoanalytic Quarterly*, 73(1), 5–46.
———. (2011). Beyond doer and done to: An intersubjective view of thirdness. In L. Aron and A. Harris (Eds.), *Relational psychoanalysis* (Vol. 4, pp. 91–130). New York: Routledge.
Berger, J. M. (2016, September 7). The toxic mix of extremism and social media. *NOVA*. Retrieved from: https://www.pbs.org/wgbh/nova/article/extremism-social-media/.
Berman, M. (2000). *Wandering God: A study in nomadic spirituality*. Albany: State University of New York Press.
Bettelheim, B. (1983). *Freud and man's soul: An important re-interpretation of Freudian theory*. New York: Knopf.
Bignold, W. (2012). The ethics of research practice: Truth through honesty. In B. McGettrick & F. Su (Eds.), *Professional ethics: Education for a humane society* (pp. 108–24). Cambridge, UK: Cambridge Scholars Publishing.
Bion, W. R. (1970). *Attention and interpretation: A scientific approach to insight in psychoanalysis and groups*. London: Tavistock.
———. (2004). *Learning from experience*. Lanham, MD: Rowman & Littlefield. (Original work published 1962.)
Bloom, A. (1987). *The closing of the American mind: How higher education has failed democracy and impoverished the souls of today's students*. New York: Simon and Schuster.
Bollas, C. (1999). *The mystery of things*. London: Routledge.
———. (2007). *The Freudian moment* (2nd ed.). London: Karnac Books.
Bos, J., Park, D., & Pietikeinen, P. (2005). Strategic self-marginalization: The case of psychoanalysis. *Journal of the History of the Behavioral Sciences*, *41*(3), 207–24. Doi:10.1002/jhbs.20101
Botticelli, S. (2004). The politics of relational psychoanalysis. *Psychoanalytic Dialogues*, *14*(5), 635–51.
Breuer, J. & Freud, S. (1956). Studies on hysteria. In J. Strachey (Ed. & Trans.), *Standard edition of the complete psychological works of Sigmund Freud* (Vol. 2, pp. 1–305). London: Hogarth Press and the Institute of Psycho-Analysis and the Institute of Psycho-Analysis. (Original work published 1895.)
Britton, R. (1992). The Oedipus situation and the depressive position. In R. Anderson (Ed.), *Clinical lectures on Klein and Bion* (pp. 34–45). The New Library of Psychoanalysis, Vol. 14. London: Routledge.
Bromberg, P. (1998). *Standing in the spaces: Essays on clinical process, trauma and dissociation*. Abingdon, UK: Psychology Press.
Carnochan, P. (2001). *Looking for ground: Countertransference and the problem of value in psychoanalysis*. Hillsdale, NJ: The Analytic Press.
Cartwright, M. (2012, November 26). Yin and yang: Definition. *Ancient history encyclopedia*. Retrieved from: http://www.ancient.eu/Yin_and_Yang/.
Chen, V. (2017). Are campus activists too dogmatic? *The Atlantic*. https://www.theatlantic.com/politics/archive/2017/07/left-sin-richard-rorty/535278/.
Cheney, K. (2016, March 3). Millennials on Trump's appeal: 'Emotion,' 'honesty.' Retrieved from: https://www.politico.com/story/2016/03/donald-trump-youth-vote-220210.
Chibber, V. (2016, November 26). *Consent, coercion, and resignation: The sources of stability in capitalism*. Lecture given in Zagreb, Croatia, organized by the Center for Labor Studies. Retrieved from: https://www.youtube.com/watch?v=2dcVoQbhFtQ.
Chomsky, N. (1999). *Profit over people: Neoliberalism and the global order*. New York: Seven Stories Press.
———. (2014). *Masters of mankind: Essays and lectures, 1969–2013*. Chicago: Haymarket Books.
Cohan, J., & Jenkins, S. (2016, October 23). *Political Freud: Blockages or new bodies, antifascism or free love? Two political-Freudian bodies in tension* [video file]. Presented at the Annual Conference of the Association for the Psychoanalysis of Culture and Society, New Brunswick, NJ.

Corbett, K. (2001). Centrality and marginality in human development. *Psychoanalytic Dialogues, 11*(3), 313–35.
Cornwell, R. (2010, October 9). Why 9 out of 10 Americans love statistics. *Independent Voices.* Retrieved from: https://www.independent.co.uk/voices/commentators/rupert-cornwell/rupert-cornwell-why-9-out-of-10-americans-love-statistics-2102408.html.
Cotto, A. (2013, January 18). American has a macho problem. *Huffington Post.* Retrieved from: https://www.huffingtonpost.com/andrew-cotto/america-has-a-macho-probl_b_2468374.html.
Critchley, S. (2007). *Infinitely demanding: Ethics of commitment, politics of resistance.* New York, London: Verso.
Cushman, P. (1995). *Constructing the self, constructing America: A cultural history of psychotherapy.* New York: De Capo Press.
———. (2005). Between arrogance and a dead-end: Psychoanalysis and the Heidegger-Foucault dilemma. *Contemporary Psychoanalysis, 41*(3), 399–417.
———. (2015). Relational psychoanalysis as political resistance. *Contemporary Psychoanalysis, 51,* 423–59. Doi:10.1080/00107530.2015.1056076.
Danto, E. (2005). *Freud's free clinics: Psychoanalysis and social justice, 1918–1938.* New York: Columbia University Press.
de Tocqueville, A. (2003). *Democracy in America* (G. E. Bevan, Trans.). London: Penguin Books. (Original work published 1835.)
Dolan, E. (2018, January 31). Study: Leftists just as likely to be dogmatic as authoritarians as those on the right. *PsyPost.* https://www.psypost.org/2018/01/study-leftists-just-likely-dogmatic-authoritarians-right-50674.
Douthat, R. (2014, May 15). The Age of Individualism. *New York Times.* Retrieved from: https://www.nytimes.com/2014/03/16/opinion/sunday/douthat-the-age-of-individualism.html.
Drassinower, A. (2003). *Freud's theory of culture: Eros, loss, and politics.* Lanham, MD: Rowman and Littlefield.
Durkheim, E. (1951). *Suicide: A study in sociology* (J. A. Spaulding, Trans., & G. Simpson, Ed. & Trans.). Glencoe, IL: Free Press. (Original work published 1897.)
Eigen, M. (2001). *Ecstasy.* Middletown, CT: Wesleyan University Press.
———. (2011). *Eigen in Seoul, Vol. 2: Faith and transformation.* London: Karnac Books.
Erlich, H. (2013). *The couch in the marketplace: Psychoanalysis and social reality.* London: Karnac Books.
Esposito, L. (2014, April 28). 11 tips to maximize your psychotherapy sessions: How to bounce off the couch quicker. *Psychology Today.* Retrieved from: https://www.psychologytoday.com/us/blog/anxiety-zen/201404/11-tips-maximize-your-psychotherapy-sessions.
Fanon, F. (2004). *The wretched of the earth* (R. Philcox, Trans.). New York: Grove Press. (Original work published 1961.)
Featherstone, L., Henwood, D., & Parenti, C. (2018, July 16). "Action Will Be Taken": Left anti-intellectualism and its discontents. *Damage Magazine,* https://damagemag.com/2018/07/16/action-will-be-taken-left-anti-intellectualism-and-its-discontents/. (Original work published in 2002.)
Ferry, L. (2011). *A brief history of thought: A philosophical guide to living* (T. Cuffe, Trans.). New York: Harper Perennial.
ffytche, M. & Pick, D., eds. (2016). *Psychoanalysis in the age of totalitarianism.* New York: Routledge.
Fisher, M. (2009). *Capitalist realism: Is there no alternative?* Winchester, UK: Zero Books.
Fong, B. (2012, March 18). Freud's radical talking [blog post]. *New York Times Opinionator.* Retrieved from: http://opinionator.blogs.nytimes.com/2012/03/18/freuds-radical-talking.
———. (2016). *Death and mastery: Psychoanalytic drive theory and the subject of late capitalism.* New York: Columbia University Press.
Foucault, M. (1975). *Discipline and punish.* New York: Random House Books.
Fraiberg, S., Adelson, E. & Shapiro, V. (1975). Ghosts in the nursery: A psychoanalytic approach to the problems of impaired infant–mother relationships. *Child and Adolescent Psychiatry, 14*(3), 387–421.

Frank, T. (2017, March 7). Millions of ordinary Americans support Trump. Here's why. *The Guardian*. Retrieved from: https://www.theguardian.com/commentisfree/2016/mar/07/donald-trump-why-americans-support.

The Free Association. (2011). *Moments of excess: Movements, protest and everyday life*. Oakland, CA: PM Press.

Freud, S. (1955). Beyond the pleasure principle. In J. Strachey (Ed. & Trans.), *Standard edition of the complete psychological works of Sigmund Freud* (Vol. 18, pp. 1–64). London: Hogarth Press and the Institute of Psycho-Analysis. (Original work published 1920.)

———. (1957a). Mourning and melancholia. In J. Strachey (Ed. & Trans.), *Standard edition of the complete psychological works of Sigmund Freud* (Vol. 14, pp. 237–58). London: Hogarth Press and the Institute of Psycho-Analysis. (Original work published 1917.)

———. (1957b). The unconscious. In J. Strachey (Ed. & Trans.), *Standard edition of the complete psychological works of Sigmund Freud* (Vol. 14, pp. 159–204). London: Hogarth Press and the Institute of Psycho-Analysis. (Original work published 1915.)

———. (1958a). The dynamics of transference. In J. Strachey (Ed. & Trans.), *Standard edition of the complete psychological works of Sigmund Freud* (Vol. 12, pp. 97–108). London: Hogarth Press and the Institute of Psycho-Analysis. (Original work published 1912.)

———. (1958b). Formations on the two principles of mental functioning. In J. Strachey (Ed. & Trans.), *Standard edition of the complete psychological works of Sigmund Freud* (Vol. 12, pp. 218–26). London: Hogarth Press and the Institute of Psycho-Analysis. (Original work published 1911.)

———. (1958c). Observations on transference-love. In J. Strachey (Ed. & Trans.), *Standard edition of the complete psychological works of Sigmund Freud* (Vol. 12, pp. 157–71). London: Hogarth Press and the Institute of Psycho-Analysis. (Original work published 1915.)

———. (1958d). Recommendation to physicians practicing psychoanalysis. In J. Strachey (Ed. & Trans.), *Standard edition of the complete psychological works of Sigmund Freud* (Vol. 12, pp. 109–20). London: Hogarth Press and the Institute of Psycho-Analysis. (Original work published 1912.)

———. (1961). Civilization and its discontents. In J. Strachey (Ed. & Trans.), *Standard edition of the complete psychological works of Sigmund Freud* (Vol. 21, pp. 57–146). London: Hogarth Press and the Institute of Psycho-Analysis. (Original work published 1930.)

———. (1962). Further remarks on the neuro-psychoses of defense. In J. Strachey (Ed. & Trans.), *Standard edition of the complete psychological works of Sigmund Freud* (Vol. 3, pp. 45–61). (Original work published 1896.)

———. (1964). An outline of psychoanalysis. In J. Strachey (Ed. & Trans.), *Standard edition of the complete psychological works of Sigmund Freud* (Vol. 23, pp. 144–207). London: Hogarth Press and the Institute of Psycho-Analysis. (Original work published 1938.)

———. (2006). *Interpreting dreams* (J. Underwood, Trans.). London: Penguin Books. (Original work published 1900.)

Fromm, E. (1950). *Psychoanalysis and religion*. New Haven, CT: Yale University Press.

Gao, G. (2015, March 12). How do Americans stand out from the rest of the world? Pew Research Center. Retrieved from: http://www.pewresearch.org/fact-tank/2015/03/12/how-do-americans-stand-out-from-the-rest-of-the-world/.

Garfinkle, M., & Steinkoler, M. (2015). The possibility of contradiction. *Division/Review, 15*, 13–17.

Geffner, A. (2006). Political identity: A personal postscript. In N. Hollander, L. Layton, & S. Gutwill (Eds.), *Psychoanalysis, class and politics: Encounters in the clinical setting* (pp. 217–24). New York: Routledge.

Gentile, J. (2015). Parrhesia, Phaedrus, and the polis: Anticipating psychoanalytic free association as democratic practice. *Psychoanalytic Quarterly, 84*(3), 589–624.

Gentile, J. & Macron, M. (2016). *Feminine law: Freud, free speech, and the voice of desire*. New York: Karnac.

Gilman, M. (2014). A court for the one percent: How the supreme court contributes to economic inequality. *University of Baltimore Law*. Retrieved from: https://scholarworks.law.ubalt.edu/cgi/viewcontent.cgi?article=1261&context=all_fac.

Goodman, D. & Severson, E. (eds.) (2016). *The ethical turn: Otherness and subjectivity in contemporary psychoanalysis*. London & New York: Routledge.
Gosepath, S. (2011, Spring Edition). "Equality," *The Stanford Encyclopedia of Philosophy*, Edward N. Zalta (ed.), URL: https://plato.stanford.edu/archives/spr2011/entries/equality/.
Gramsci, A. (1971). *Selections from the prison notebooks*. New York & London: Lawrence and Wishart. (Original work published between 1929 and 1935.)
Gregg, M. (2016, November 13). The productivity obsession: In today's always-on workplace, employees crave any app that promises a chance at regaining control over their time. *The Atlantic.* Retrived from: https://www.theatlantic.com/business/archive/2015/11/be-more-productive/415821/.
Gregoire, C. (2014, March 20). How happiness became a cultural obsession. *Huffington Post.* Retrieved from: https://www.huffingtonpost.com/2014/03/20/happiness-self-help_n_4979780.html.
Gunn, D. (2019, January 16). Why racial economic disparity keeps growing in the U.S. Pacific Standard. *Pacific Standard.* Retrieved from: https://psmag.com/economics/why-racial-economic-disparity-keeps-growing-in-the-us.
Habermas, J. (1989). *The structural transformation of the public sphere*. Cambridge, MA: MIT Press.
Haidt, J. (2012). *The righteous mind: Why good people are divided by religion and politics.* New York: Random House.
Harcourt, E. (2013). The place of psychoanalysis in the history of ethics. *Journal of Moral Philosophy*, *12*, 598–612. Doi:10.1163/17455243-4681030.
Harlem, A. (2015). Dignity in three acts. *Psychoanalytic Dialogues*, *25*(4), 452–62.
Harvey, D. (2005). *A brief history of neoliberalism*. Oxford, UK: Oxford University Press.
Hawkes, D. (2003). *Ideology*. New York: Routledge.
Hayek, F. (1960). *The Constitution of Liberty*. London: Routledge and Kegan Paul.
Heidegger, M. (1962). *Being and time*. New York: Harper & Row. (Ralph Manheim, Trans.). (Original work published in 1927.)
———. (2002). *On the essence of truth: On Plato's cave allegory and Theaetetus* (T. Sadler, Trans.). New York: Continuum Books.
———. (2010). *Country path conversations*. Bloomington: Indiana University Press. (Original work published 1959.)
Herman, E., & Chomsky, N. (1988). *Manufacturing consent: The political economy of the mass media*. New York: Pantheon Books.
Herron, W. (1995). Development of the ethnic unconscious. *Psychoanalytic Psychology*, *12*(4), 521–32.
Hertz, D. (2014, August 13). One of the best ways to fight inequality in cities: zoning. *Washington Post.* Retrieved from: https://www.washingtonpost.com/posteverything/wp/2014/08/13/the-best-way-to-fight-inequality-in-cities-is-through-zoning/?utm_term=.c12c1adf74d1.
Hollander, N., Layton, L., & Gutwill, S. (Eds.). (2006). *Psychoanalysis, class and politics: Encounters in the clinical setting*. New York: Routledge.
Horgan, J. (2019, February 18). Revolt against the rich. *Scientific American*. Retrieved from: https://blogs.scientificamerican.com/cross-check/revolt-against-the-rich/.
Horkheimer, M., & Adorno, T. W. (2002). The culture industry. In G. S. Noerr (Ed.) & E. Jephcott (Trans.), *The dialectic of enlightenment: Philosophical fragments* (pp. 94–136). Stanford, CA: Stanford University Press. (Original work published 1944.)
Howitt, R. (2001). Frontiers, borders, edges: liminal challenges to the hegemony of exclusion. *Geographical Research, 39*(2), 233–45.
Hutchison, E. D. (2012). Spirituality, religion, and progressive social movements: Resources and motivation for social change. *Journal of Religion & Spirituality in Social Work*, *31*, 105–27. Doi: 10.1080/15426432.2012.647891.
Jacoby, R. (1983). *The repression of psychoanalysis*. Chicago: The University of Chicago Press.
Johanssen, J. (2019). *Psychoanalysis and digital culture: Audiences, social media, and big data*. New York: Routledge.

Kantor, J. & Streitfeld, D. (2015, August 15). Inside Amazon: Wrestling big ideas in a bruising workplace. *New York Times*. Retrieved from: https://www.nytimes.com/2015/08/16/technology/inside-amazon-wrestling-big-ideas-in-a-bruising-workplace.html.

Khan, M. (1979). *Alienation in perversion*. New York: International Universities Press.

Khanna, R. (2003). *Dark continents: Psychoanalysis and colonialism*. Durham, NC: Duke University Press.

Khzmalyan, E. (2015, January 27). Living in America: lets talk about individualism. *The Armenite*. Retriteved: from http://thearmenite.com/2015/01/living-america-lets-talk-individualism/.

Kirsner, D. (2000). *Unfree associations: Inside psychoanalytic institutes*. Lanham, MD: Rowman and Littlefield.

Klein, M. (1935). A contribution to the psychogenesis of manic-depressive states. *International Journal of Psycho-Analysis*, *16*, 145–74.

———. (1940). Mourning and its relation to manic-depressive states. *International Journal of Psycho-Analysis*, *21*, 125–53.

Kovel, J. (1981). *The age of desire: Reflections of a radical psychoanalyst*. New York: Pantheon Books.

———. (1983). *The age of desire: Reflections of a radical psychoanalyst*. New York: Random House Inc.

Lacan, J. (1992). *The ethics of psychoanalysis, 1959–1960*. New York: W.W. Norton. (Original work published in 1986.)

Lakoff, G. (2004). *Don't think of an elephant! Know your values and frame the debate*. White River Junction, VT: Chelsea Green.

———. (2006). *Thinking points: Communicating our American values and vision*. New York: Farrar, Straus & Giroux.

Layton, L. (2006). Attacks on linking: The unconscious pull to dissociate individuals from their social context. In N. Hollander, L. Layton, & S. Gutwill (Eds.), *Psychoanalysis, class and politics: Encounters in the clinical setting* (pp. 107–17). New York: Routledge.

———. (2009).Who's responsible? Our mutual implication in each other's suffering. *Psychoanalytic Dialogues*, *19*(2), 105–20.

———. (2010). Irrational exuberance: Neoliberal subjectivity and the perversion of truth. *Subjectivity*, *3*(3), 303–22.

———. (2014). Grandiosity, neoliberalism, and neoconservatism. *Psychoanalytic Inquiry*, *34*(5), 463–74.

———. (2015). Beyond sameness and difference: Normative unconscious processes and our mutual implication in each other's suffering. In D. Goodman and M. Freeman (Eds.), *Psychology and the Other* (pp. 168–88). New York: Oxford University Press.

———. (2016). Yale or jail: Class struggles in neoliberal times. In D. Goodman & E. Severson (Eds.), *The ethical turn: Otherness and subjectivity in contemporary psychoanalysis*. London & New York: Routledge.

Lear, J. (1998). *Open minded: Working out the logic of the soul*. Cambridge, MA: Harvard University Press.

Louden, R. (1989). Some vices of virtue ethics. In L. Pojman (Ed.), *Ethical theory: Classical and contemporary readings* (2nd ed., pp. 311–20). Belmont, CA: Wadsworth.

MacIntyre, A. (1981). *After virtue: A study in moral theory*. London: Gerald Duckworth.

Maleen, M. (2018, November 12). The competitive personality then and now. *Damage Magazine*, https://damagemag.com/2018/11/12/the-competitive-personality-then-and-now/.

Marcuse, H. (1955). *Eros and civilization: A philosophical inquiry into Freud*. Boston, MA: Beacon Press.

Mason, L. (2018). Ideologues without issues: The polarizing consequences of ideological identities. *Public Opinion Quarterly*, 82(1), 280–301. https://doi.org/10.1093/poq/nfy005.

McGowan, T. (2016). *Capitalism and desire: The psychic cost of free markets*. New York: Columbia University Press.

McLaughlin, N. (2001). Optimal marginality: Innovation and orthodoxy in Fromm's revision of psychoanalysis. *Sociological Quarterly*, *42*(2), 271–88.

McMillan, D. W., & Chavis, D. M. (1986). Sense of community: A definition and theory. *American Journal of Community Psychology*, *14*(1), 6–23.
McWilliams, N. (2004). *Psychoanalytic psychotherapy: A practitioner's guide*. New York: Guilford Press.
Menand, L. (2019, January 28). The supreme court case that enshrined white supremacy in law. *The New Yorker*. Retrieved from: https://www.newyorker.com/magazine/2019/02/04/the-supreme-court-case-that-enshrined-white-supremacy-in-law.
Merleau-Ponty, M. (2012). Phenomenology of perception (D. Landes, Trans.). New York: Routledge. (Original work published 1945.)
Mill, J. S. (2001). *On Liberty*. Kitchener, Ontario, Canada: Batoche Books Limited. (Original work published in 1859.)
Mills, J. (2012). *Conundrums: A critique of contemporary psychoanalysis*. New York: Routledge.
Mindell, A. (2002). *The deep democracy of open forums*. Charlottesville, VA: Hampton Roads.
Mitchell, J. (2016, March 17). Equality: A hope without a party. *American Interest*. Retrieved from: https://www.the-american-interest.com/2016/03/17/equality-a-hope-without-a-party/.
Mitchell, S. (1988). *Concepts in relational analysis*. Cambridge, MA: Harvard University Press.
Moss, D. (2003). *Hating in the first person plural*. New York: Other Press.
———. (2016). Our crying planet: An approach to the problem of climate denial. *Psychoanalytic Quarterly*, *85*(1), 189–97.
———. (2018). *At war with the obvious: Disruptive thinking in psychoanalysis*. New York: Routledge Press.
Nietzsche, F. (1974). *The gay science, with a prelude in rhymes and an appendix of songs* (W. Kaufman, Ed. & Trans.). New York: Random House. (Original work published 1887.)
———. (1999). *The birth of tragedy* (R. Geuss & R. Speirs, Eds., R. Speirs, Trans.). Cambridge, UK: Cambridge University Press. (Original work published 1872.)
Nozick, R. (1974). *Anarchy, State, and Utopia*. New York: Basic Books.
Nussbaum, M. (1999). Virtue ethics: A misleading category? *Journal of Ethics*, *3*(3), 163–201.
Ogden, B. H., & Ogden, T. H. (2012). How the analyst thinks as clinician and as literary reader. *Psychoanalytic Perspectives*, *9*(2), 243–73.
Ogden, T. (1992). Comments on transference and countertransference in the initial analytic meeting. *Psychoanalytic Inquiry*, *12*(2), 225–47.
———. (2001). Conversations at the frontier of dreaming. *fort da*, *7*, 7–14.
———. (2004). This art of psychoanalysis: Dreaming undreamt dreams and interrupted cries. *The International Journal of Psychoanalysis*, *85*(Pt. 4), 857–77.
———. (2005). What I would not part with. *fort da*, *11*, 8–17.
Oliver, K. (2004). *The Colonization of psychic space: A psychoanalytic theory of oppression*. Minneapolis, MN: University of Minnesota Press.
Orange, D. (2009). Psychoanalysis in a phenomenological spirit. *International Journal of Psychoanalytic Self Psychology*, 4(1), 119–21.
———. (2010). Recognition as: Intersubjective vulnerability in the psychoanalytic dialogue. *International Journal of Psychoanalytic Self Psychology*, 5, 227–43.
———. (2016). *Climate crisis, psychoanalysis, and radical ethics*. Oxford & New York: Routledge.
Parsons, M. (1999). The logic of play in psychoanalysis. *The International Journal of Psycho-Analysis*, *80*(5), 871–84.
Peltz, R. (2005). The manic society. *Psychoanalytic Dialogues*, *15*(3), 347–66.
The Pew Center for People and the Press. (2009, May 21). *Trends in political values and core attitudes: 1987–2009* [Report]. Retrieved from: http://people-press.org/files/legacy-pdf/517.pdf.
Phillips, A. (2012). *Missing out: In praise of the unlived life*. New York: Farrar, Straus & Giroux.
Piety, M. G. (2004). The long term: Capitalism and culture in the new millennium. *Journal of Business Ethics*, *51*(2), 103–18.
Pulcini, E. (2013). *Care of the world: Fear, responsibility, and justice in the global age*. New York: Springer Science and Business Media.

Putnam, R. (2000). *Bowling alone: The collapse and revival of American community*. New York: Simon and Schuster.
Racker, H. (1966). Ethics and psycho-analysis and the psycho-analysis of ethics. *The International Journal of Psychoanalysis*, *47*, 63–80.
Reich, W. (1970). *The mass psychology of fascism* (V. R. Carfagno, Trans.). New York: Farrar, Straus & Giroux. (Original work published 1933.)
Rorty, R. (1998). *Achieving our country: Leftist thought in twentieth-century America*. Cambridge, MA: Harvard University Press.
Rozmarin, E. (2007). An other in psychoanalysis. Emmanuel Levinas's critique of knowledge and analytic sense. *Contemporary Psychoanalysis*, *43*, 327–60.
———. (2014, August 11). Talking about Gaza in Psychoanalysis. *Public Seminar*. Retrieved from: http://www.publicseminar.org/2014/08/talking-about-gaza-in-psychoanalysis/#.WIKNJYWcE2y.
Rubens, J. (2009). *OverSuccess: Healing the American obsession with wealth, fame, power, and perfection*. Austin, TX: Greenleaf.
Ruiz-Junco, N. (2013). Feeling social movements: Theoretical contributions to social movement research on emotions. *Sociology Compass*, *7*(1), 45–54.
Rushkoff, D. (2019). *Team Human*. New York: W.W. Norton.
Saad, L. (2013, January 3). Americans consider individual freedoms nation's top virtue. *Gallup*. Retrieved from: http://www.gallup.com/poll/159716/americansconsider-individual%20freedoms%20nation-top-virtue.aspx.
Sachs, J. (2011). *The price of civilization: Reawakening American virtue and prosperity*. New York: Random House Books.
Samuelson, R. (2012, July 3). Is the U.S. a land of liberty or equality? *Washington Post*. Retrieved from: https://www.washingtonpost.com/opinions/is-the-us-a-land-of-liberty-or-equality/2012/07/03/.
Sandel, M. (1982). *Liberalism and the limits of justice*. New York: Cambridge University Press.
Sennett, R. (1998). *The corrosion of character: The personal consequences of work in the new capitalism*. New York: W. W. Norton.
Shedler, J. K. (2010). The efficacy of psychodynamic psychotherapy. *American Psychologist*, *65*, 98–109. Doi:10.1037/a0018378.
Stepansky, P. (2009). *Psychoanalysis at the margins*. New York: Other Press.
Stern, R. D. (1983). Unformulated experience: From familiar chaos to creative disorder. *Contemporary Psychoanalysis*, *19*(1), 71–99.
Stiglitz, J. (2013, February 16). Equal opportunity, Our national myth. *New York Times*. Retrieved from: https://opinionator.blogs.nytimes.com/2013/02/16/equal-opportunity-our-national-myth/.
Stolorow, R. D. (1988). Intersubjectivity, psychoanalytic knowing, and reality. *Contemporary Psychoanalysis*, *24*(2), 331–37.
Streeck, W. (2017). *How will capitalism end?* London, New York: Verso Books.
Subvert. (n.d.). In *Vocabulary.com dictionary*. Accessed June 9. Retrieved from: https://www.vocabulary.com/dictionary/subvert.
Subvert. (2017a). In *Dictionary.com unabridged*. Retrieved from: http://www.dictionary.com/browse/subvert.
Subvert. (2017b). In *The Free Dictionary.com* . http://www.thefreedictionary.com/subvert.
Subvert. (2017c). In *Merriam-Wesbter.com dictionary* (11th ed.). Retrieved from: https://www.merriam-webster.com/dictionary/subvert.
Summers, F. (2013). *The psychoanalytic vision: The experiencing subject, transcendence, and the therapeutic process*. New York: Routledge.
Taplin, J. (2017). *Move fast and break things: How Facebook, Google and Amazon have cornered culture and what it means for all of us*. New York: Little, Brown and Company.
Tauber, A. I. (2010). *Freud: The reluctant philosopher*. Princeton, NJ: Princeton University Press.
———. (2012). Freud's social theory: Modernist and postmodernist revisions. *History of the Human Sciences*, *25*(4), 43–72.

Teicholz, J. G. (2001). Chapter 2: The many meanings of intersubjectivity and their implications for analyst self-disclosure and self-expression. In A. Goldberg (Ed.), *The narcissistic patient revisited: Progress in self-psychology* (Vol. 17, pp. 9–42). Hillsdale, NJ: Analytic Press.

Thompson, M. G. (1995). *The truth about Freud's technique*. New York: New York University Press.

———. (2004). *The ethic of honesty: The fundamental rule of psychoanalysis*. Amsterdam, The Netherlands: Rodopi.

———. (2017). *The death of desire: An existential study in sanity and madness* (2nd ed.). New York: Routledge.

Tolentino, J. (2017). The gig economy celebrates working yourself to death. *The New Yorker*. Retrieved from: https://www.newyorker.com/culture/jia-tolentino/the-gig-economy-celebrates-working-yourself-to-death.

Verhaeghe, P. (2014, September 29). Neoliberalism has brought out the worst in us. *The Guardian*. Retrieved from: https://www.theguardian.com/commentisfree/2014/sep/29/neoliberalism-economic-system-ethics-personality-psychopathicsthic.

Viner, K. (2016, July 12). How technology disrupted the truth. *The Guardian*. Retrieved from: https://www.theguardian.com/media/2016/jul/12/how-technology-disrupted-the-truth.

Volkan, V. (2014). *Psychoanalysis, international relations, and diplomacy: A sourcebook on large-group psychology*. London: Karnac Books.

Wachtel, P. L. (2010). Beyond "ESTs": Problematic assumptions in the pursuit of evidence-based practice. *Psychoanalytic Psychology*, *27*, 251–72. Doi:10.1037/a0020532.

Wampold, B. E. (2005). The psychotherapist. In J. C. Norcross, L. E. Beutler, & R. F. Levant (Eds.), *Evidence-based practices in mental health: Debate and dialogue on fundamental questions* (pp. 200–207). Washington, DC: American Psychological Association.

Walls, G. (2004). Towards a global critical psychoanalysis. *Psychoanalytic Dialogues*, 14(5), 605–34.

Wallwork, E. (1991). *Psychoanalysis and ethics*. New Haven, CT: Yale University Press.

Weber, M. (2001). *The Protestant ethic and the spirit of capitalism* (T. Parsons, Trans.). London: Routledge. (Original work published 1904.)

Weintrobe, S. (2013). *Uneasy Relationship with the Natural World: Engaging with Climate Change: Psychoanalytic and Interdisciplinary Perspectives.* New York: Routledge.

Westen, D., Novotny, C. M., & Thompson-Brenner, H. (2004). The empirical status of empirically supported psychotherapies: Assumptions, findings, and reporting in controlled clinical trials. *Psychological Bulletin*, *130*(4), 631–63.

Whippman, R. (2016, December 22). America is obsessed with happiness—and it's making us miserable. *Vox.* Retrieved from: https://www.vox.com/first-person/2016/10/4/13093380/happiness-america-ruth-whippman.

White, G. (2017, May 16). Getting to the Bottom of American's Fascination with Wealth. *The Atlantic*. Retrieved from: https://www.theatlantic.com/business/archive/2017/05/greenfield-generation-wealth/526683/.

Williams, J. (2016, November 10). What so many people don't get about the U.S. working class. *Harvard Business Review*. Retrieved from: https://hbr.org/2016/11/what-so-many-people-dont-get-about-the-u-s-working-class.

Winnicott, D. W. (1960). *The theory of the parent—infant relationship. International Journal of Psycho-Analysis*, *41*, 585–95.

———. (1965). *Maturational processes and the facilitating environment: Studies in the theory of emotional development* [PDF]. Retrieved from: http://www.abebe.org.br/wp-content/uploads/Donald-Winnicott-The-Maturational-Process-and-the-Facilitating-Environment-Studies-in-the-Theory-of-Emotional-Development-1965.pdf.

———. (1971). *Playing and reality*. London: Tavistock.

Wolff, R. (2016, April 27). How capitalism and racism support each other. *Truthout*. Retrieved from: https://truthout.org/articles/how-capitalism-and-racism-support-each-other/.

Zaretsky, E. (2015). *Political Freud: A history*. New York: Columbia University Press.

Zepf, S. (2010). Psychoanalysis—on its way down a dead-end street? A concerned commentary. *Journal of the American Academy of Psychoanalysis and Dynamic Psychiatry*, *38*(3), 459–81.

Zuboff, S. (2019). *The age of surveillance capitalism: The fight for a human future at the new frontier of power*. New York: Hachette.

Index

About the Author

Amber Trotter, PsyD, completed her bachelor's degree in sociology at Middlebury College. Her senior thesis focused on social movement theory and climate activism. She received her doctorate from the California Institute of Integral Studies, where she currently teaches. She completed her clinical internship at the Access Institute. She is a founding editor at *Damage Magazine* and thinks and writes about psychoanalysis, ethics, politics, digital technology, and processes of social change. She is in private practice in Healdsburg and San Francisco.

www.ingramcontent.com/pod-product-compliance
Ingram Content Group UK Ltd.
Pitfield, Milton Keynes, MK11 3LW, UK
UKHW041122071026
15587UKWH00009B/76

9 781498 573320